N O W

# LAUREN

# BACALL

# NOW

CENTURY

First published by Century in 1994

Copyright © Lauren Bacall 1994

Lauren Bacall has asserted her right under the Copyright, Designs and Patents Act, 1988, to be identified as the author of this work

First published in the United Kingdom in 1994 by Century Random House UK Ltd, 20 Vauxhall Bridge Road, London SW1V 2SA

Random House Australia (Pty) Limited
20 Alfred Street, Milsons Point, Sydney
New South Wales 2061, Australia

Random House New Zealand Limited
18 Poland Road, Glenfield
Auckland 10, New Zealand

Random House South Africa (Pty) Limited
PO Box 337, Bergvlei, South Africa

Random House UK Limited Reg. No. 954009

ISBN 0 7126 3011 2

Photographic Credits
7, 14, 21, 40, 44, 45, 48, 127, 147 (top and bottom), 153, 158, 164, 181 (top), 181 (bottom), 186, 189 From the private collection of Lauren Bacall; 15 Bob Smith/Laura Gaiza; 18 Paramount Pictures; 19 Warner Brothers; 25 Alan Berliner; 28 Courtesy Patrick Demarchelier; 38 (top and bottom) Martha Swope, © 1994; 53 (top) Capitol Studios, Hartford, Conn.; 53 (bottom) Phil Stern; 58 Mikki Ansin; 60 Phil Stern; 66 Central Press Photos, London; 70 Theo Westenberger; 93 Courtesy Allen M. Schneider, Associates; 127 Abner Klipstein; 138 Henri Dauman; 143, 144 John Haynes; 169 Robert Millard, © 1982; 172 Christina Burton; 176 John Engstead; 203 Mikki Ansin

Composed by Dix, Syracuse, New York
Printed and bound by Quebecor Printing Martinsburg, Martinsburg, West Virginia

To friendship, the relationship I value above all others,

And for my friends—past and present.

I have loved and do love you all.

# CONTENTS

Acknowledgments

This book could not have been written without the aid, patience, encouragement, and advice of my editor, Victoria Wilson; the friendship and fresh eye of Robert Gottlieb; the generous ear of Bill Loverd; the help, devotion, understanding, and wit of my friend and great assistant, Bonni Kurt; and the support of Sonny Mehta and all the empty offices and rooms of my publisher, Alfred A. Knopf, whose occupants lent me their space and bade me welcome.

I thank you, thank you, thank you and embrace you all.

# NOW

# INTRODUCTION

This book is, well, let me tell you first what this book is *not*. It is *not* a chronological autobiography to follow *By Myself*—my last book. It is *not* a sequel. It *is* about life: what has filled the last fifteen years, experiences that have shaped me. Work I have done—how it has affected my life, what it has given me, what, as I see it now, reflecting on the years between forty and sixty, it might have taken away. How, having reached this point in life, I am forced to face my body's inability to accomplish all that I have taken for granted through the years, though I have to tell you, it's held up pretty well. How work will determine, more than ever, the way I live now and how I want to live for all my tomorrows. How I have closed off a part of myself and have continued to live alone. People I have known, time I have lost. Friendships: how they change and how they never change. What absence does to them; what being a solo female does to them. The growing of my children and my relationship with them. The arrival of grandchildren. The changes in me. My awareness of my own mortality and trying to figure things out.

The people I have chosen to write about are people who are important to me. They are people who have taught me—changed me—made me laugh, cry, feel—each remarkable in his or her own way. They have been in my mind and heart for many years, so much so that there was nothing for me to do but put them on paper. That is the *why* of this book, these are the subjects—these and the perceptions and misconceptions, the problems, the possibles, and the actuals in this misshapen world that have shaped me.

L ife is amazing, life is odd. Life is not what you expected it to be. Things happen, people enter your life; some take it over, some try to. Growing up takes longer than you think. I always thought I was so smart. Now that I have reached the advanced middle years—passed them, truth to tell —I have discovered an extraordinary happening. Something that came upon me—unplanned, unsought after, unsuspected. I must preface my finding the light at the end of the tunnel with the following observations.

People's perceptions of me have always been thorns in both my sides. It's not so much that I care what they think—though I fear I do, some of them anyway. It's that I am seen by many as the combination of roles I played in movies; my early persona, oft repeated in newspapers and magazines as part of the Howard Hawks–Warner Bros. hype—and my marriage to Humphrey Bogart and how I was said to have changed him (untrue: he changed himself); and my years of saying what I think in my professional and private life—directly. Bogie always did. Having never had a flunky to precede me—to pave the way, set the stage, do the heavy work, the dirty work, to make sure that all was as it was supposed to be—I've been doing it myself, telling the truth. Well, my truth at any rate. Bogart did that too. A chancy thing to do in a world that is not used to hearing the truth and not crazy about hearing it when it's told. All these things, plus my voice, which has been one of my better features. One of the things I had that Howard Hawks wanted me to keep—that made me somewhat special. It's deep, you see. And we won't go into the number of times I have been called mister on the other end of the telephone.

And I have noticed increasingly through the years, that when a man speaks his mind it is accepted as charming, interesting, sexy, but when a woman speaks hers she is aggressive, unattractive, pushy—some might even say a bitch. But I digress. The fact is, it is not my custom to say terrible things, to insult. It is my custom to speak my mind. And I fear I must admit that there have been times when I wished I had remained silent.

I was brought up by my mother, and we lived with my grandmother for many years. I went to a girls' boarding school and a girls' high school. So I grew up believing that women had the upper hand—got things done—were listened to. In some homes I guess they still are. And also are the power behind the you-know-what. It's women I admire more—for character, honesty, daring, courage, curiosity, chance taking, general bravery about life—but it's men who get the quick action. And from where I sit, it doesn't look as though that's going to change. Oh, I think they're trying now, and one or two tiny steps forward might have been taken. The glimmer of a breakthrough. I hope.

I have come to realize something else—astounding, understandable, yet quite marvelous in its way. I met Humphrey Bogart when I was nineteen years old. I married him when I was twenty, and that marriage lasted for eleven and a half years. So for twelve and a half years he was, among many other things, my teacher. He taught me his philosophy of life. He taught me the rules of the Hollywood game. He taught me the usage and abusage of actors, called stars by the press, which couldn't have cared less what happened to any of us. It was good copy, true or not, that mattered most. We were expendable —he taught me that too. He taught me about standards and the price one must pay to keep those standards high. He taught me about the value of work and the importance of truth and character. Though I must honestly say I had been raised by my mother and my Uncle Charlie on these same principles. But Bogie continued where they left off.

Bogie was a favorite of the press because he was good copy and they enjoyed what he said. They would not have enjoyed it half so much had I said it. When quoting him (not often correctly) it was sometimes "he snarled," but more often "he said"—whereas with me it has more often been "she barked" instead of "she said." Over the years I have come to realize that being a chameleon by nature and instinct, during our marriage I began to take on some of his traits. Not only because they were so dazzling and such fun, but because of the verbal games he and I played. And from the day of his death—and more and more—his teachings have permeated my being. With each passing year I find myself repeating more and more often to my three children and to many of my friends his words of wisdom. Because they were true more than forty years ago, when he said them, and it's more necessary that they be said and heard today, now that we have been drowning in mediocrity for too many years. And so the realization that I have been dealing with people very much in the Bogart tradition has come up and hit me squarely between the eyes. And the discovery that I have been carrying it on for a long, long time, is that how two become one and is that one way people live on after death? In Bogie's case, of course, he lives on—will live on through film.

So it seems to me I have been dealing with people very much in the Bogart tradition. My great discovery is that I am carrying it on, and have been for a long, long time. I must have figured if it was okay for him, it would be okay for me. Is that one way people live on after death? In Bogie's case, of course, he lives on as an actor through film, but through me he lives on as Bogie (and this is the correct spelling)—as I knew him, and as I hope will continue with our children, Steve and Leslie, and with my son Sam as well.

I find that when I am commenting about something, I inevitably hear, "Why don't you tell us what you really think?" No one ever asked Bogie that question. Why me? Is venturing an opinion

Happy days on the *Santana*, around 1948. We could not have been steering from that position: we were obviously happily becalmed.

such a bad thing—is saying what you think dangerous? I was taught to contribute to a conversation, to think and to say what I think—the truth—out loud. Anyway, I have no choice. I'm a lousy liar.

Another misconception—people assume that having worked all my adult life, I must be rich. Wrong! And having been married to a big star like Bogart, I must be very rich. Wrong again on both counts. Then what follows? Being rich, why does she work? Why not, for God's sake? What do you do with your life if you don't work? Why is it the American dream to work really hard when you are young so you can retire early? Why can't it be that you work for love of it— or to get better at it? Isn't it incongruous to work like a dog for three quarters of your life so you can stop and enjoy the rest? How do you know what there will be to enjoy? Why do we Americans yearn for vacations instead of fulfillment? For shorter workweeks—yet more pay? Why should we get paid for working less? Somewhere along the line the message has been misdirected, goals have changed. The priority has become money, not quality, not the texture of life. We miss so much in our American quest for things.

As long as you are able, why stop being productive, making a contribution? What are we all here for, anyway, if not to do that? Surely it's better to sleep late in the morning only when it's a rare privilege, not an everyday occurrence.

All that and the realization that the core of Bogie resides in me is what has taken these many years to surface. It fascinates me—it makes me smile. It's the way it is and the way it will be. And because of the strength of it—the value of it and the power and influence of him in what turned out to be my still formative years—what I have learned demanded to be committed to paper, to be shared now.

# WORK

From childhood I have lived with and been surrounded by people whose main purpose seemed to be work. Not purpose in life, really, but driving force, I suppose—fulfilling need. My mother, my Uncle Charlie, almost all my relatives; Bogie, Huston, Jason, almost all my friends. It was unquestionably the most natural way to go.

You work because you love it, because you want to and because you need to, even if the part you're offered is not quite what you hoped for. In fact, it almost never is. But the fact that it's work means, first of all, that you'll be occupied—busy—have a reason to get up in the morning; and, second, that financial obligations will be met, some of the pressures will be off. You'll be using yourself and learning something, no matter how simple or less than starring the part seems to be. And best of all, you'll be doing what you've been trained to do.

So it began for me. I couldn't wait to finish school so I could pursue my life's goal—to be an actress. Work. It meant independence and being on my way to dream fulfillment. Interesting that my first big break—the biggest of my life, the break to make all my dreams come true—should be the one that would force me to put work second. I fell in love with and wanted to marry Bogie as badly as I wanted to breathe. That meant making a promise to him that I would not take location jobs—jobs that would take me away. Our life together would come first. No matter what. It did, and though there were many moments of career frustration for me, our life was more important. And thank God I made that choice. But in spite of it, in our house, work was always present.

When Bogie died, work moved back into first place in my life. Fortunately, all through my marriage I had kept a thread of it alive, enough not to be forgotten. Otherwise I don't know *what* would have happened to me. What I'd have done.

Yet when I married Jason Robards I went right back into the old pattern: not going on location; marriage, children first. My career began to shift then, with more focus on the stage, and as home was New York, the place to work was not so much a problem. Of course, life and the acting profession being what they are, I did get offers for work outside New York. And since the work I do comes in spurts, I've spent a great deal of my life in a state of angst. Though I confess I have a feeling that angst is a natural state with me.

It's hard to turn down work. I remember being offered a movie in Mexico with Kirk Douglas and Rock Hudson. It would have meant two or three months away from Jason and my three children (Sam was then two or three). I wanted it all, but I couldn't have it all. So I chose home and family. The part I said no to was not a great part, but it was in a good Western, with good people and I would have enjoyed being in it. I just couldn't bring myself to leave. If there had been a way for me to make the movie in my living room—ah, that would have been perfect! But perfect is not part of life's pattern. Certainly not mine.

Something kept my name alive. I found myself, even with the changes in the entertainment world, continually doing something. Those changes I speak of were mostly television. My awareness of that kept me active. I have too much energy to do nothing and too much curiosity, imagination, and ambition to stop acting. And I love it. I feel good doing it, though every now and then the thought passes quickly through my brain: how long will I be *able* to do it? Will I ever be on the stage again? Can I still be good at it? I don't dwell on any of this, because I don't have time, because it is not a fascinating way to spend my days, and because I don't really want to entertain even the possibility of not being able to function at something I've given the better part of my life to. I want to be like John Gielgud, who at the very ripe age of ninety is still delivering the goods, and brilliantly. One thing I am convinced of is that the more you do, the more you can do. So I don't let up. I won't let up.

I n the Seventies I had not been deluged with acting offers in any of the performing arts. These years were not the most productive or prolific in my acting life. They were years of readjustment, of finding my place after two years in England, of becoming part of my profession in my own country again. It was a period of uncertainty, of learning, of trying to stabilize.

I got through that time by appearing as a guest on game shows, doing the occasional commercial. It was writing my autobiography that saved me, that provided me with a goal. (And in some basic way, it gave me a way of life, gave me direction, and reawakened the writing section of my brain that had been lying dormant for so many years.)

When you're in the working mode, when all of you—your head, your senses—is pointed in that direction and there is no work for you, it is not only unsettling, it submerges you in almost total negativity. Is this it? Are you at the end of your career? Will those creative juices never flow again? That is when your strength—will—confidence must be forced to the surface. That is when you must invent new avenues for your talent—must expand your horizons if you are to prevail.

• • •

It was in the spring of 1977 that I decided I needed a break from writing my first book. I was into the last part of my life at that point (only on paper, fortunately), so I decided to take a musical on a summer tour. I desperately needed to perform, to be on a stage again. The show was *Wonderful Town*. Originally starring Rosalind Russell, it was based on the play *My Sister Eileen*, and the book and lyrics were written by Betty Comden and Adolph Green, the music by Leonard Bernstein. It had been a big hit way back then, when it was done on Broadway, and Roz Russell was, of course, superb.

We were to open the Dallas Music Fair and play for two weeks The rest of the tour would encompass the Valley Forge Theater in Pennsylvania; the Westbury Music Fair on Long Island; the St. Louis MUNY, an outdoor theater seating more than ten thousand people and always played in the deadly heat of a Missouri summer with cottonballs from onstage trees falling into eyes, ears, and mouth; and Miami, the final stop. The first two theaters were in the round, a new experience for me. Plus which I'd never done a summer tour before. So it was another plunge into the unknown, always an irresistible temptation.

Arvin Brown, who was a friend of long standing and a first-rate director, agreed to use the hiatus from his Long Wharf Theatre in New Haven to direct his first musical. Peter Gennaro, a successful and respected, not to mention talented, dancer and choreographer, was to choreograph. Then came the casting. I had the right to approve. It's always been odd to me that one actor can have approval of another. The main reason for that clause in a contract is to protect the star from a producer's going after the cheapest instead of the best, to keep the high standard flying, and to make certain that the leading man and other principals will be the best possible and will work well together. Of course, that's something you never know until you're in the middle of it and it's too late, though I have found that for the most part, the better the actors, the easier they are to get along with.

This would be only my second musical, and I have always believed that the road to a successful musical or successful anything is paved with first-rate talent. We were lucky; after several indecisive auditions, Arvin said he knew the perfect man for the lead, George Hearn. So this wonderful actor and marvelous singer, previously unknown to me, had to stand in a rehearsal hall in broad daylight (summer packages do not have the luxury of a darkened theater for auditioning) and sing.

Here we were in this brightly lit rehearsal hall, with one large table separating us—Arvin and me on one side, George on the other. And George—opera trained—standing there, certainly feeling exposed and vulnerable, having to audition for a summer package, if you please, not even Broadway. I marveled at his ability to stand there and deliver. As I sat listening to his song, in my discomfort I thought again how very brave actors are. How the baring of our souls never ends—still needing and hoping for approval, in the knowledge that more often than not it is rejection that plays the starring role in an actor's scenario.

Luckily, we ended up with a super cast. It was a twelve-week tour, short but very sweet. Yul Brynner, having gone that route with *The King and I*, had told me to beware of shin splints; running or walking up and down the aisles is hell on your legs. In the round, it is an uphill climb from stage to dressing room. And it is the oddest feeling to be standing at the top of an aisle—in character, mind you —waiting to make an entrance. Picture this: As you must enter on cue, you are obliged to move down the aisle slowly and early and must try not to be noticed by the audience on either side of you, not to distract, yet concentrate, focus on the scene and arrive onstage on cue, never breaking the mood. Not easy. Of course, the more I did it, the more at ease I became. Finally it was kind of fun (the theater is almost always fun, though I admit I prefer a proscenium to the round).

Even in a summer package, which by its very nature must

This picture was taken on my book tour en route to Australia in 1980.

Traveled a lot while in the round in *Wonderful Town*. It was 1977.

be scaled down from Broadway, the excitement can and should be and in this case *was* there. Lucky for me to have been able to play in *Wonderful Town*—a strong book, magnificent score. I loved doing it, though one night I did have an unnerving experience. Betty Comden and Adolph Green came to the Westbury theater, and though we have been the closest of friends for many years, business is business—they were still the writers, and I am always more nervous when I know who's out front. To compound the nightmare, Leonard Bernstein was there too. It's tough enough for a nonprofessional singer to sing in a musical, but with the composer present it's horrendous. I almost fainted when he appeared in my dressing room, old friend or no. He thought my performance was fine, except (God—that word) for one note, of which he wasn't too fond. Well, neither was I, so we were even. It's moments like those that lead you to say to yourself: *Why* am I here? *Why* do I put myself through this? Am I *sure* I want to continue in this profession? No matter how many years—how much experience —I have never found a way to conquer sensitivity to judgment. Where, oh where, is that mythical prince on the white horse—now —when I need him?

My son Sam, then fifteen years old, came down to Pennsylvania to visit me before going off to camp. More juggling of my personal life, more being torn between home and the need, both emotional and financial, to work. I wanted my son with me. We had become so close in the years since my divorce from his father. He filled so many empty spaces in my life and was the best company in the world.

The road can be very lonely. Strange cities, hotels, impersonal rooms. I find myself almost totally dependent on members of the company. The easiest time is after the show, when the natural thing for most of us is to go for a drink and a hamburger at the best of the local eateries. During the day it's a bit more difficult. You often find yourself alone. I'm not very good at inviting myself. Also, the rest of the company often feel they don't want to impose on the star of the show or think you want to be alone or have other things to do. As a rule, none of that is true, but it takes a long time to get the message across.

Every time I start a tour, it's as though I'm doing it for the first time. I forget how to pack, what to pack. Then again, that's true of me everywhere I go. And given the fact that more and more of my life is spent moving from one place to another, you'd think I'd have packing down to a science. No such luck.

Always when a tour is coming to an end there is sadness. Endings are invariably painful, especially for a theatrical company that has been together for a solid three to four months. It doesn't seem a long time, but it is in the theater. There is much exchanging of phone numbers. You don't want to lose track of one another. You want to keep that thread alive, you mean for it all to continue. So in the midst of farewell parties, drinks, laughter, hugs and kisses, there is always an underlying sadness. You have bared yourself on a stage before strangers and in a rehearsal room, you've had your good nights and your bad nights and your stomachaches, you've seen each other in a way you haven't been seen before. It's all special—unique to that time.

After the last performance of *Wonderful Town* I gave a farewell party in my hotel suite. We all took off the next day for points east and west. Our farewell was slightly drunken, though there was food, of course—I am manic about planning the menu, having too much of everything just in case. We are sentimental, some of us, trying to hang on to our make-believe world a little longer despite knowing how futile that is. Then facing the suitcases for one final bout of packing. When those cases are closed and we head for home, we head for a period of adjustment, another feeling of displacement. Certainly the fact of having been away from home, friends, family for months is part of it. Telephone contact is not enough. It's never enough.

I feel so estranged from everyone when I come home. It's hard for me to call and say, "I'm back"—it always sounds to me as though I'm waiting for an invitation, and in a way I suppose I am. I want to be back in the fold again. But they've become used to my absence, so they have to readjust as well. We almost pick up where we left off, but not quite. Eventually I get back in stride, at least enough to feel at home in my house and see my friends again after the first awkwardness has passed, and to get back to my writing routine, which I dearly love.

Need, need, will you never go away? Though I guess that's a bad wish, for without it I would stop, full halt, no speed ahead.

I seem to be split, or more than that, quartered. Is there a movie—is there a movie for television—is there a play—is there something? Something to demonstrate

A happy photo, though Duke had little to laugh about, 1977.

that I can still do it, that I can deliver more than before, that I won't just disappear? That this vacuum that I feel now will be filled.

When you're in a play, the movie world stops thinking of you. They—the multi and invisible "they"—figure, Oh, she's in a play, she doesn't want to make movies anymore, *if* they even think that. So you are automatically eliminated from their thoughts when casting time comes up.

But, and this is often the case, just as I was convinced the movie world had forgotten me permanently, I was offered *The Shootist* with John Wayne. It was the story of a man dying of cancer and how he dealt with his last days. John Wayne *was* dying of cancer, so of course the movie had special meaning for him; it gave me remarkable insight into this surprising man. I'd worked with Duke years before in *Blood Alley*—strangely enough, the year Bogie was diagnosed with

*Blood Alley* days, 1956. Great looking guy.

cancer. *The Shootist* was really all about Duke, the man in the story. My part was all right, not great, but it was an opportunity I was not about to pass up. It was, sadly, Duke's last movie. We had a high-altitude location for a few days, which didn't help his breathing. But there was nary a whimper from him. Duke really was a frustrated director, and he'd comment on the camera setups and move the actors around. He was ornery, but then he had always been ornery. At the same time, he had incredible sweetness. I knew he felt rotten all the time or most of it, but he never complained. Once he said, "God, I can't smoke anymore, can't drink anymore, all the fun's gone," a sentiment I was to hear from John Huston many years later. Men like Duke and John were so macho, it drove them mad not to be able to do what they had always done. But finally, because they wanted to live, they stopped smoking and they stopped drinking.

My son Sam came out to California for his spring vacation while we were filming. He came on the set one day, and while the crew was lighting the scene he stood in front of Duke, coming up to his chest. Duke put his hand affectionately around Sam's head, cupping his chin; to this day Sam remembers Duke's hand, so huge it almost covered his face.

One day Duke and I were shooting a scene, and while waiting for the final adjustment of the lighting he took my hand ever so gently and just held it. An act of warmth and friendship. One of the crew said, "Boy it's a beautiful day!" Duke's response was "Every day you wake up is a beautiful day." Said simply, matter-of-factly, it was a killer line, spoken by a brave and terrific man. I could totally disagree politically with someone like Duke, we would never move in the same circles, have the same interests, friends—yet I could really connect with him, care about him, even be attracted to him.

During the last half of the filming, my stepfather, Lee, called and told me that my Uncle Bill, my only uncle by marriage, was going into the hospital. His kidneys were failing and he had to be put on a dialysis machine. He started it and didn't like it, but he had to have it; he would die without it. Yet he wanted to disconnect. My Uncle Bill was a man who had pretty much always followed his own star. A lawyer who should have been a teacher, he was wedded to detail, the kind of man who when driving to a particular location would give us (the children) a map so we could follow our route and know where we were. When I was a little girl, I spent many weekends with him, his wife, who was my mother's sister Renee, and my cousins Judith and Joan, whom I was very close to. I was quite frightened of my Uncle Bill then. When

Uncle Bill—always happy surrounded by books—in his early seventies.

his rich, full-bodied voice echoed displeasure, I wanted to hide. He was a man of moods, a lover of classical music and whiskey who, as it turned out, was secretly sentimental. He loved his children and he loved me, but I never heard him say it. Not in so many words. When I became a success in *To Have and Have Not*, he wrote me a lengthy letter telling me how happy he was for me, how proud, but that I must never forget how much my mother had sacrificed for me, how little she had cared for her own life in her pursuit of mine. How all my growing-up years she had put her personal life on hold in order to give me all the opportunities life might offer.

I had always been aware of my mother's support of me in any road I chose to follow, but like most children I took it somewhat for granted. Bill's letter made me stop and think some more. Not only about her but about him and his awareness of her. It was the kind of letter I would not have expected from him. Now that I think of it, I got a letter similar in tone from my almost surrogate father, my Uncle Charlie. I see how much they loved my mother and how perceptive about human nature they were to realize how quickly the young move on with their own lives, leaving their parents behind.

After hearing about Bill's condition, I called my Aunt Renee. They had been semi-separated for years, though they went on living together—he at one end of the apartment, she at the other, a unique and funny arrangement.

She told me she had gone to see him in the hospital daily and had just sat with him. He'd wanted her to. Here was a pair of people who were married over half a century, with problems for maybe twenty of those years, yet who went on living together, albeit at opposite ends of an apartment; people whose interests were quite different, yet who shared a profound emotion: love of their children and grandchildren. They had loved each other once—God knows what they had shared, had been through, before finally leading their separate lives under the same roof. Yet in his final days, she sat with him and he wanted her with him. I said he must not be allowed to take himself off the dialysis machine, to which she replied, "But you know how stubborn he is." She gave me his phone number, and the next day I called him during my lunch break. I begged, pleaded, cajoled: "You must not do this, someone will come along with a new discovery, a simpler way to deal with your problem. Please, Bill, there's so much still to enjoy and do in life. Please wait for me to come home; at least that. I'll be finished shooting soon. I'll come straight home. Please." "You're sweet," he said. "You've always been sweet, but I can't. No. It's time to say goodbye." I couldn't believe it. I was dissolved in tears. I'd never known anyone to make such a choice. Renee stayed with him to the last. What guts he had! My cousins, though naturally terribly upset, were strangely accepting of his decision, knowing, I suppose, that they had no choice. But I couldn't figure it out. How could you say it's time to leave this world? How could you not try everything to stay alive? I had no answers. I could not persuade him; he'd said goodbye. That was a new kind of loss for me. Perplexing, infuriating, devastating. But how I admired him!

I returned home and dove back deeply into my first book, not to emerge until it was done.

• • •

When in 1980 *Woman of the Year* as a musical was broached to me by my good friend Peter Stone, I was immediately interested. He got a copy of the movie starring Katharine Hepburn and Spencer Tracy—two people I loved—and ran it for me one night. My first reaction was that the movie was perfect, that Kate and Spence were perfect, and how dare anyone try to improve on perfection. But Peter had his own ideas, and after much back and forthing, and to and froing, we got together a first-class group of creative artists. John Kander and Fred Ebb of *Cabaret*; *New York, New York*; *Zorba*; *Chicago*, and many other shows would write the score. Robert Moore, who had acted with me in *Cactus Flower* fourteen years earlier and had since become a successful director of Neil Simon plays and musicals, to direct. My great friend the great designer Tony Walton to do the sets; Tony Charmoli to choreograph; Don Pippin, who had been musical director for me in *Applause*, to repeat his performance here. Then, as I always do, I started to train like a prizefighter. So with the one, the only, Keith Davis—who has seen me through every play from *Cactus Flower* on —singing lessons, daily exercises, body stretches, etc., began. You have to be in physical shape to be in a musical. No one who hasn't had the experience can possibly know the amount of energy and stamina required.

Though I have been in the theater in a serious way for more than thirty years, from *Goodbye Charlie* to *Applause* to *Woman of the Year* to *Sweet Bird of Youth*, WOTY was only my fourth Broadway experience. It's that I've been, in the words of my friend John Gielgud, "one of those actresses who stay in a play for a long time." Two years in *Cactus Flower*; five years, including Broadway, touring, and London, in *Applause*; two and a half years in *Woman of the Year*. Indeed, I have stayed for a long time. In musicals, I have felt obliged to stay because they are so much more costly than straight plays and therefore take longer to get back their initial costs and go to profit for the investors.

Auditions progressed, with Peter Stone, Kander and Ebb, Robert Moore, Don Pippin, and me—sitting low in my seat in the theater so the auditioning actors wouldn't see me. It's a process that seldom shows an actor at his best—you're on trial, for God's sake. You want the job. You're nervous. If you were confident going in, that confidence often leaves once you start your audition.

When we planned the national tour of *Woman of the Year*, we had a new director, Joe Layton, who along with me insisted on certain changes. Bob Moore was involved with another project by then. It was my first meeting with Joe Layton, a magical, creative man who became a great friend. We fell in love instantly, though not romantically. He came into the rehearsal period with a fresh eye, and since he was a choreographer as well as a director, musicals were his meat. Joe had the great gift of encouragement and appreciation—I can honestly say he brought out the very best in me and inspired all the people he worked with. It was a great time for me, almost like doing a whole new show. Peter Stone and Kander and Ebb wrote some terrific new material, my voice seemed to be better than before (I had stopped smoking during rehearsals). We opened in Los Angeles, where I have my daughter and many friends, and we were to stay there for two and a half months, so I was happy.

Rehearsal time is always the best time for an actor. It's a time of discovery, of opening yourself up layer by layer, of finding things, inventing, creating, learning. Musical comedy may seem easy to do and lacking much depth of emotion, but that is a misconception. As an actor you still have to find the basic truth of the character you're playing and your relationships to and with the other characters in the play. Comedy has always been more difficult to play than drama. Comedy, if you think about it, is almost always based on truth and generally serious concepts. And timing—that you either have or you don't: it is timing that rules the day. Luckily, that is my one God-given gift, and I treasure it. One of the greatest compliments I've ever been given was when Jack Benny told me I had perfect timing.

A completely fresh approach to a show that had played on Broadway for over a year and a half was a fascinating exercise. I couldn't wait to get to rehearsal every morning. I couldn't work hard enough or long enough. I have always been a hard worker, dedicated to what I am doing, but this experience happened at a time in my life when I was emotionally fragile. And there is no single reason that I can give. I felt alone, very alone, and very vulnerable. Partially, I suppose, because Sam, my last child, in whom I had invested so much love and laughter, so much plain, ordinary pleasure, was clearly on

With dear Joe Layton, who made this tour a more rewarding experience than Broadway. *Woman of the Year*, 1983.

his way out of the nest. He was involved with a girl who I did not feel was the right girl for him in any way and who had tremendous influence over him. I know that we mothers never think the mates our children choose are good enough. We see things that they don't, we know the pitfalls, we want them to avoid the pain of our failures. We want them to know what they are or might be, so they'll recognize it themselves. But they don't and they won't, and there's not a thing we can do about it. I've always prided myself on being the most modern of mothers. I know the score, I've been around enough. As Bogie used to say, "I've seen everything, done everything." I hoped I would be fair about my children's choices. First of all, just as I did, they will do as they please anyway, and so they should. I want to be friendly with their mates and what I really care about is their happiness and our continuing relationship.

Yes, at the time of the *Woman of the Year* tour I was fragile. Cried easily, was moodier than usual, hypersensitive, not my usual fun-loving, cover-up self. My humor has never completely left me, luckily, but I desperately needed someone to lean on. I chose Joe Layton—my soul mate, my new best friend. The fact that he had an entire show to deal with, not to mention a life and problems of his own, seldom crossed my mind.

Joe was around as much as he could be. Of course, once a show has opened, the director's job is done; he must go on to the rest of his professional life and back to his private one. All understood logically by the likes of me, but not emotionally. But he was there all of our Los Angeles time and part of our San Francisco time and kept in telephone touch after that. Now he too is gone—this man of endless creativity, with whom I was in perfect harmony, gone—another empty space.

At the time of the show, I was in the midst of another trauma that was of no help to my fragile state. That involved Blenheim, my beautiful Cavalier King Charles spaniel, who had been with me almost constantly since I bought him in London in 1973. The only time I was without him was when I went overseas; the rest of the time he traveled with me on planes, trains, and automobiles, slept on my bed, was my companion. When Blenheim was seven, my vet discovered that he had an enlarged heart. He went along quite well in the beginning, no particular symptoms, but before leaving for the tour in California, the vet discovered that his heart had grown to a potentially dangerous and alarming degree. He gave me medication, a letter explaining Blenheim's physical problems, age, etc., all in veterinary terms, plus a list of doctors in each city of the tour. I was terrified. Blenheim was a great theater dog, stayed in my dressing room, never made a sound, knew when I was onstage. I told him, of course, that he had to be quiet, and being a great dog, he understood.

It was about halfway through the L.A. tour that I noticed Blenheim seemed listless; when he wanted to jump up on my bed, he would try but couldn't, and he'd whimper until I'd lift him onto the bed. But carefully, because if I picked him up the least bit carelessly he would let out a yell. I knew he wasn't right, so I took him to a veterinary hospital in Westwood. They had impressive facilities, but I didn't like the place. It was cold, the natives were not overly friendly, the doctor himself was remote. If you've ever had a sick dog, you know that friendliness and warmth are essential to dog and master.

Blenheim had to stay for continued observation: his heart was definitely not good; he had arrhythmia plus high blood pressure. (Funny how I'd never thought of his or any other dog's blood pressure —stupid of me.) "Could I see him?" "No, better let him stay quiet for another day." I was so worried he would be worse away from me, especially in foreign, unfriendly surroundings, that I stopped by after the show to see for myself. They said he was resting, they'd given him something to keep him quiet; it wasn't good for him to get excited. If he saw me he would think I was going to take him home. I would have to wait.

The ghastly thing about dealing with a dog rather than a person is that you can't reason with it, explain to it that a separation is only temporary, that it's not being deserted. After another day it was determined that Blenheim might have had a slight heart attack; he

27

Although Blenheim is not smiling, he was healthy in this photo, 1977.

must stay in the hospital until his heartbeat and all vital signs were stable. I went to see him, talked to him, stroked him. He looked so sad, very quiet, accepting his lot. After a week they let me take him home, but the prognosis was negative. After another X ray, the vet held out little hope for my much-loved companion. He was unsubtle in giving his diagnosis—no bedside manner, cold. I'd have to watch Blenheim closely; his heart was so large it was getting harder and harder for him to breathe and move. God, losing a friend is painful, and he was a friend, my best. That old theatrical tradition—leave aches and pains and personal problems in the dressing room—still applies. We were closing in L.A., moving to San Francisco. That would not change. So I had to wrench myself from the sadness of my beloved companion and focus on the fact of the tour. I *had* to get ready—I *had* to organize the kitchen of life. The sooner I did that, the sooner I could give my attention fully to Blenheim.

Pack-out day on a show, particularly a musical, is always fraught—mixed emotions, leaving familiar dressing rooms, backstage, feeling unsettled again. Each new city is an unknown quantity. No matter how many times you've been there, if it's a new show, with new audiences, you cannot predict the outcome. By the middle of the last week in a city, you begin slowly packing your own clothes; all electricals in your hotel must be packed and picked up before the final day. The propman—and for *Woman of the Year* we had a great one, Munro Gabler—always coordinated with me and did everything to simplify my life. Notices for the company go on the backstage board during the last two weeks: hotel reservations for the next stop, pickup days for trunks, things traveling on the prop truck. It's complicated, there's a great deal to synchronize, it gets done, but it ain't easy. In actual fact it turns out to be kind of fun. An adventure—leaving the old and comfortable for the unknown new. Also, despite distances between cities, despite travel time changes, the props must get to the next stop when the sets do, or preferably before. That it works as well as it does is a tribute to the backstage pros, without whom the show simply would *not* happen.

San Francisco is a city I adore—beautiful, fun, great weather, a terrific hotel, the Huntington, with its view of the beautiful bay. And the staff was very welcoming to me and my dog, a big plus. I made an appointment with the recommended vet to check Blenheim, and arrived at his office with X rays and a full history. Luckily, the man turned out to be every dog or animal owner's dream of what a vet is supposed to be. First and foremost, he loved animals, and I saw it immediately by the way he behaved with mine and the way Blenheim responded. He knew immediately he was in a friendly environment, so he relaxed. I left him for a few hours to be examined while I had my orchestra rehearsal.

That's another difference between musicals and straight plays. Soon after arrival at every stop, while the crew is hanging the show—which means setting backdrops, sets, props, etc.—before the technical rehearsal there is an orchestra rehearsal. Not in the theater necessarily; usually in a rehearsal hall set up for that purpose. On a major tour you carry four or five key musicians, depending on what the traffic (meaning the producers) will bear, plus of course the most important to me, the conductor. The rest of the orchestra consists of local musicians, who must learn the score, rehearse with the conductor first, then play through for the actors.

On a tour, the only hiatus you have is no hiatus, one day between opening in one town and closing in another. You close on a Saturday night, Sunday is travel day—sometimes Monday if you're lucky—then you open Tuesday or Wednesday, usually Tuesday. You have orchestra rehearsal Monday afternoon and the technical—that's lighting, working the sets—Monday night, followed by a dress rehearsal the next afternoon and the opening that night. If there's time, you get to run through your numbers in the theater, on a darkened stage. I love this part. I feel that it's my bonding time with that theater, that it's mine, that it belongs to me, so it's very special. Because each

theater is different in size and shape, the acoustics change, therefore
the orchestra may sound different to us onstage and we may sound
different. So that kind of rehearsal, no matter how rough, is a great
help, a necessity. Also, from an actor's point of view, even with empty
seats you get a sense of what the theater will feel like. There's really
no explaining it. It has to do with aura. The life each theater has had
—plays and people that have given it life—affects an artist's response.
It's one of the things that make the live theater such a special place. It
may sound hokey to think of all the major actors, the theatrical greats,
who might have graced various stages, but they are what gives each
one its particular patina and vibes. It's exciting for any performer—
any lover of the stage and its lore—to think that Ethel Merman might
have sung *Annie Get Your Gun*, or *Gypsy*, or even her first show, *Girl
Crazy*, at the Golden Gate in San Francisco, or that Alfred Lunt and
Lynn Fontanne or Helen Hayes or any theater legend might have
played on its stage.

San Francisco turned out to be pivotal for Blenheim. The
prognosis remained negative, even with this wonderful vet. I was told
that with his heart history, Blenheim was lucky to have been alive as
long as he had, that there was nothing really that could be done for
him but to keep him as comfortable and happy as possible. One day
at a time. The vet said he was a beautiful, gallant dog, and the important thing for me to remember and think about was the quality of
his life.

After my last trip to the vet, I never let Blenheim out of my
sight except when I was onstage. One night after the show I was on
my hotel bed watching television, with Blenheim lying next to me. I
remember putting my head on my pillow and him getting so close to
me he almost wrapped himself around my neck. Finally I was able to
get into a breathing position. He was so adorable—he lay alongside
me, cheek to cheek, licking my face from time to time. At last I was
able to sleep, though not deeply, not restfully. I felt him moving
during the night to the middle of the bed, then to the foot, then he
was almost on my face again, until finally sleep again. Suddenly a

piercing scream unlike anything I had ever heard. I quickly sat up in bed. No Blenheim. I looked around, to find him on the floor, moaning. I ran for the nitroglycerin pills, forced one into his mouth, which was nearly locked, almost impossible to open. I called the vet, who said to get him right over there—it sounded like a heart attack. It was seven in the morning. I carried my poor Blennie downstairs. By this time he was a bit more comfortable. I was terrified and shaking badly. I was afraid to move him too much, for fear I'd make it worse. Getting in and out of the taxi was not easy—he was heavy—but we finally made it to the hospital. The vet took him immediately into an examining room, allowing me to come in and watch. There was no fooling around this time: Blenheim had indeed had a serious attack. Even so, he cried when I left the room. I suppose he was afraid he wouldn't see me again. What torture! After giving instructions to his assistant, the vet sat me down with a cup of coffee, warning me that it was now clear this sort of thing was going to happen more often, that my pet's heart could not take too much more and that his courage more than anything else had kept him alive. Intellectually I could face it all, but emotionally—not a chance. I certainly could not give up as long as Blenheim continued to fight.

Next stop Seattle, and Blenheim became listless, started to lose weight. The heart attacks had taken their toll. I tried to comfort him, but I had been warned in San Francisco that it would all be downhill now. There was no way to prepare. It seemed to happen suddenly. He had difficulty standing, more difficulty lifting his leg; I had to hand feed him a good deal of the time and even then I couldn't get him to eat much. One day he'd perk up a little, and the next he'd lapse into quiet lack of interest; an occasional cry would emerge, indicating a sudden pain or just the effort of moving. I held him and stroked him, spoke softly to him. I hope my presence helped, but he was fast removing himself from his world and mine.

There was one bright moment during the Seattle part of the tour. That was Thanksgiving, when my darling son Sam was able to spend a few days with me. I hadn't seen him in several months and knew he would boost my spirits. He always did. Of course, he could not accept the possible demise of Blenheim. The young always seem to think that life never ends. If only!

I missed my children, I missed them a lot. I'd had my daughter, Leslie, with me for almost three months in Los Angeles, and she came up for a weekend in San Francisco. The *Santana*, Bogie's beautiful sailboat of the perfect hull, was now living at the San Francisco Yacht Club, under the ownership of two super brothers, Ted and Tom Eden. They'd invited me aboard and to the yacht club. It was not sailing weather, and I couldn't have sailed during the week anyway, with eight shows to play. But oh, it was a strange, nostalgic, bittersweet feeling to see and climb aboard the *Santana* after almost twenty-five years. Bogie's presence was strongly felt when I sat in the cockpit and went below. So many pictures of him, of me, of us together flashed before my eyes. There is a myth about my distaste for sailing. Untrue! My frustration was that we could never go anyplace else, because the boat was there, and expensive, and the only place other than home that Bogie really wanted to be. In fact, I loved being on it—just the two of us. No skipper. I love the water—I love to swim —but I don't enjoy (or rather my stomach doesn't enjoy) rough seas. The Edens adored the boat, raced her as she was meant to be raced, and in waters where Bogie had always wanted to race her. They generously offered their time to Leslie so that she could see the *Santana*, see what had meant so much to her father. I yearned for her brother Steve to be there too, but he couldn't be. As he had spent some time on board with his father, I am sure that if he had been able to just sit in the cockpit, through osmosis more memory would be jarred back to life.

Steve was the child I had been most apart from in the last ten years or so, largely because he had married so young, become a father so young, and lived in Connecticut. Steve, my cherished firstborn, the one to carry on the Bogart name, was so damaged by his father's death and subsequent rebirth to cult status that he spent his early adult years hiding from that legacy. Understandable. How do you measure up to a paragon of perfection? How can you be a hero when your father was a hero of such giant proportions that you can only fade in that reflected presence? It took him a while, but he finally found his place. I always knew he would be the best at what he chose to do; he was the one who didn't know it. He knows it now. And he is so much his father's son that it's almost eerie. I was impatient with Steve, I wanted him to deal with his past, present, and future immediately, all at once. I wanted him to know everything I know. Well, as almost everyone I've ever known, myself included, has had to, he had to do it in his time and his way. It took me too long to realize that. I was being driven by my emotions, which, despite my supposed capability to reason, I seem to work from most of the time. I talk a reasonable, logical game, but it's my gut that gets it every time.

As Seattle was drawing to a close, Steve Ross's office at Warner's, who were one of the backers of the tour, made arrangements to have the Warner plane take me to St. Louis, the next stop on the tour. There I would leave Blenheim with the local vet, who had generously offered to keep him at his home. I would then go to Chicago for a two-day visit with Joe Layton, who was presenting a musical revue in a large nightclub. It was just before Christmas, so there was snow and ice. But it was Chicago, a marvelous city, a cheerier atmosphere than my next two stops would be—and a break from the show, from routine; the first break I'd had in more than seven months.

I love the theater. I love being onstage, I even enjoy touring —new faces, new sounds, new colors, new everything—but after playing a show for a year and a half on Broadway, then touring for another year, it is time for a change. And it's not necessarily the show that needs changing; it's the routine. At the same time every day you must wake up, have breakfast; at the same time you must vocalize, get to the theater, do your body warm-ups, then start your makeup; and at the same time the curtain goes up and, usually, comes down. It's the nagging sameness of the routine that has gotten to me in the past.

When it hits you, you feel trapped, locked in a vise—and in a sense you are. That is why it's necessary to be in a good hotel, to be comfortable. You have to have a sense of going to sleep and waking up in a cozy, friendly atmosphere. Not possible in some cities, but so essential.

When I arrived in St. Louis from Chicago, the gloom of the sky matched the gloom of the hotel room. I had to go directly to the theater, but I called the vet, who said that Blenheim was definitely failing. I asked if I could come to see him after the dress rehearsal that night. Eleven or eleven-thirty p.m. is late for a man to be receiving when his day starts at seven a.m., but fortunately for Blenheim and for me, this was a lovely and caring man. I was nervous and scared. The doctor and his wife greeted me at the door and led me to a dimly lit room, where, next to a radiator, lay Blenheim, covered with a blanket. He barely moved. I leaned over him, gently hugged him, kissed him, and talked to him. He managed to lick my face, but not energetically. He was too sick, too tired. I gingerly lifted him onto my lap. He had gotten so small, so frail. I just stroked him, talked to him, over and over and over. He did not respond in any visible way. No tail wagging, no raising of his head, but he knew it was me and knew I was there. I didn't really think that he was dying. I just stayed with him, sitting on the floor with him on my lap, stroking him. I felt I couldn't keep the vet up any longer, so finally, after a lingering farewell to my loving companion of ten years, I left, saying I'd return the following day. We had two previews the next day, but I would get to the vet's between shows, come hell or high water. I called in the morning: no change. Before making an entrance in the first act, I noticed our company manager on the phone. I knew. At the intermission I cornered her. "I saw you on the phone—Blenheim." "Yes," she said. "I wanted to wait till the end of the show." But I had known —had known even before I saw her on the phone. I called the vet. Blenheim had seen me, felt me; he couldn't hang on any longer. I couldn't believe it, so final, so painful. And I wasn't with him. I thought of those other, more devastating endings. Though I was asleep in the next room, I wasn't with Bogie; and though I was at her side, I wasn't with my mother. I didn't get a chance to say the last-minute things I would have wanted to say. You hear about those who sit by their loved one's bed, holding their hand, watching them slowly slip away. Well, it never happened to me that way. Born alone—die alone.

I don't know how I got through the second act, how I got through the day, except that I did, I had to. I went to the vet's house to collect Blenheim's collar and leash. You know the way you do those things—not seeing, not feeling, in a daze. I moved so aimlessly after that. I couldn't concentrate on anything except when I was onstage and had to, and even that was an effort. I had to call my children to tell them. Sam was the most affected because he had chosen Blenheim, he was there from the beginning.

I kept going, of course—walked and talked, ate, even laughed—but I refused to think of having another dog. Though being alone was now lonelier than ever, there was no replacement for that particular Cavalier King Charles spaniel.

I gave a Christmas party for the company in Detroit. I had planned it in San Francisco, had bought favors for the boys and girls. A musical on tour means a company, a large company; not a cast of five or six actors or even eight or ten, but a nucleus of anywhere from thirty-five to fifty people. There's not only the onstage company: actors, singers, dancers; there's the backstage company: props, crew, stage managers, assistants; the front-of-house people: company manager, lighting people, and the very important musical contingent; plus assorted wives, husbands, and significant others. I gave the party in my suite: food supplied by the hotel, drinks, and grab bag with small gifts. It was pointed out to me from the beginning—my first out-of-town tryout in *Applause*—that the ideal way to keep a company together and not isolate myself was to gather everyone together now and then. I hosted my first party after our last Saturday night in Detroit, and did we all have fun! As we probably spend more time with one another than with anyone else, we should enjoy offstage hours together as well as those onstage. It's especially important when you're out of town—keeps up company morale and mine as well. It gets lonely out there. I continued this practice even after we opened in New York. More regularly for the principals. It kept us close, in touch with one another. You know, more waking hours are spent in the theater than at home, particularly on matinee days. In the interest of self-preservation, I never leave the theater on matinee days. Food is ordered and brought in after the afternoon performance, and then I sleep for an hour. I used to go out, but it's not a wise move. First of all, you're in a public place, which means noise and people and cigarette smoke, all bad for the voice. It becomes paramount to protect your voice, which is your livelihood. And it's tiring to sit in restaurants. Since you're putting out total energy for the matinee and have to do the same thing for the evening performance, rest is numero uno. As I said, self-preservation. *After the show is my time to howl.*

I couldn't wait for the *Woman of the Year* tour to end. I'd lost my dog, I was away from home, I was physically and mentally tired after seventeen years of almost continuous stage work. I needed time to regroup. I never felt more alone. And, I admit, I might even have felt just the tiniest bit sorry for myself. My credo has been to put on a happy face. Unfortunately, there are times when that doesn't work, and this was one of those times.

When I get like that—which has not been too often, but it has happened—I almost always think travel will solve my problems. By travel I mean London or Paris. You'd think after all the packing and unpacking on a tour I'd have had enough, but packing for Europe and packing for a tour are not the same. And with all my restlessness and anxiety to move on, the fact was that when this tour ended in Chicago I did not have another job to go to. And it was another ending. Two negatives against one positive.

I'm one of the girls who's one of the guys in this picture.

The Broadway creators at the start of *Woman of the Year*, 1989.
The first day of rehearsal.

The next-to-last stop after Detroit, before Chicago, had been four weeks at the Kennedy Center in Washington. Not only do I have good friends there, but I love the city. It is beautiful and—right or wrong, good or bad—important decisions are constantly being made there. And I had not been in a city of old friends for too long. Washington housed Ann and Art Buchwald, friends of, dare I say it, more than forty years now. Our friendship began in Paris in 1951, the year of *The African Queen*. It continued through every trip to Europe and subsequently here. The Buchwalds had lived in Paris, worked there; Art's writing career as a major columnist began there. He and Bogie were a funny combination. Bogie was a first-rate chess player and he loved the game; it suited his mathematical brain. And Art loved to play too. He had a chess set in his office at the then Paris *Herald Tribune*, which was ideal for Bogie, who enjoyed having a place to go after lunch where he could do something so familiar. He often played at home, even alone, with a book of master games: he would sit and play both sides, the black and the white, and learn from doing it. I was always riveted by that—the picture remains crystal clear, even today—Bogie sitting on the sofa with a large wooden chessboard on the table, chessmen properly arranged, book of master games to his left. Bogie thinking—thumb and forefinger on chin. I had never seen anyone do that before. I have never seen anyone do it since. Art was a good player, but I have a feeling Bogie was better. Sorry, Art.

While I was playing the show in Washington, Ted Kennedy planned an evening. He bought lots of tickets for friends and people in his office, and gave a dinner at the Kennedy Center, with not only a toast to me but acknowledgment of my son Steve, who had come to visit for a couple of days. Ted also arranged for his son Ted junior to take us on a tour of the House, the Senate, the Supreme Court. He's extraordinary with friends and their children; nothing is too much trouble for him. And there is no public figure I know of who has done more or as much fighting for the rights of the elderly, for national health care, for human rights. I am and will always be indebted to Ted Kennedy, for his friendship, his support of the arts, and his public

Devil-may-care Uncle Charlie looking spiffy and healthy in his
summer suit, 1955.

stand on issues not always popular but essential to our country, to our conscience.

My four weeks in Washington lifted my spirits, so I headed for Chicago and the windup of *Woman of the Year* in a fairly light-hearted state. We were booked into the Arie Crown, following on the heels of an automobile show. The Arie Crown is not a theater. It is a convention hall, a home for boat and auto shows, but definitely not a theater. Four thousand people at least. Now, how can you communicate a joke, much less an emotion, when you look like a spot on the stage? Hopeless.

Not a happy ending for a tour. Though I wanted it to end, I wanted to go on enjoying the exchange between audience and actor. I still wanted to feel that communication, that connection with other human beings. But it is incredibly frustrating to try to be personal in a totally impersonal atmosphere. How can an audience have even a clue about a story, about relationships—how can they feel *anything*—when they're so far away? Yul Brynner had warned me about that barn, and he at least was in *The King and I*, which was much more a spectacle than *Woman of the Year*. Hard to believe what actors have to deal with, the elements involved. No matter how impenetrable the atmosphere, how high the mountain, how cold the glacier, how empty the house, we must cut through all that and play the play. Make the audience believe in love, laughter, and the life of those of us onstage. It's our job, and how cozy and warm and alive it is when performed in a normal-sized theater. But how different—what a struggle when playing in a cavernous space. Yet we must remember, no one ever said it: theater, film, in town, out of town, living, loving—life— would be easy.

My mother's work (as executive secretary in a large corporation) kept her active and involved with people, made it possible for her to get out of the house, to be in contact with the outside world. It kept her from stagnating. It doesn't matter so much that she had to work to support me, though that was a definite necessity. What does matter is that it gave her a reason to get up in the morning, it gave her a life independent of the kitchen, and it kept me aware all through my young life that work was a part of life, as much a part of life as eating and sleeping. That awareness had a great deal to do with my having goals, of my not wandering aimlessly. I couldn't have spent my life wandering aimlessly. I can't even imagine it.

I don't want to give the impression that my family were so driven by work that they did nothing else. They were a fun-loving group, with all the difficulties that varying needs and differing personalities create. They were great laughers, my Uncle Charlie the best laugher of all—and the best giver of laughter. I have a bronze head of him just outside my bedroom door. I say good morning to him almost daily and have a continuing sense of his presence; he might almost be watching over me. He died thirty-three years ago, and I still miss him and feel a tremendous pang whenever I think of him, which is often. It was so perfect that he and Bogie liked each other on first meeting.

After nineteen years of family indoctrination, at twenty I married a man who loved his work. And Bogie's main thought and yearning throughout his illness was only for work. If he could just work, he knew he would be well. After his death, I would have gone mad without work, and throughout ghastly emotional lows, work has sustained me, saved me. When I married Jason, I saw how important work was to him, how it helped him weather his life's storms. And all of my friends, the same. I have seen how lost the one or two friends of mine are who don't have a job except that of home and husband, and who can't fill their days when that home is broken. My stepfather, Lee, after my mother died, could not have survived had he not had his office to go to, to be the center of. I believe I am incapable of spending much time with anyone who doesn't work. The thought of filling my days with lunches, shopping, endless social functions, fills me with dread. Where would my energy go? Where would my humor go? How could I live if I were unable to reach out even now to try to grab the gold ring? The answer is I couldn't.

# CHILDREN

I have spent the better part of my life working (the time before that was spent growing up, and that was done quickly): working part-time—watching my mother work, Uncle Charlie work—and dreaming of the day I would be on my own and working full-time.

I was the light of my mother's life, and she was the light of mine. Yet I couldn't wait to get away, be independent. I was an only child. She had spent her grown-up life working to support me and to give me everything I needed to prepare me for my chosen profession. I needed her. I needed to know she was there for me, and she needed me to be the focus of her life.

Through Bogie's courtship of me, of which she heartily disapproved, she was there. Through my Howard Hawks problems, she was there. She never failed me. She was there to cook my breakfast, wake me to go to the studio, walk the dog, help me to choose my wedding outfit. And though she took a job in England for close to a year, she depended on me emotionally; she never said it, but I knew it. I was her priority. I was her raison d'être. When Steve's

I must have been fifteen judging from the hideous hair; my
mother looked young and lovely, and was both, 1940.

nurse died, as Bogie and I left for Europe for *The African Queen*, my mother stopped her life to go to California and look after Steve until he joined us in London. After a tentative beginning, Bogie adored her and she him—so much so that on her yearly trips to California she was at our house almost daily for the month or two that she was there. When I moved to New York, I once again depended on her, and even though she had married again and loved her husband deeply, there was no one who came before me. Yet when I went through emotional bad patches during my second marriage I didn't want her around every Sunday. I was too nervous, too tense, and I didn't really want her to see my unhappiness. Mind you, Jason Robards,

In my mother's apartment, before or after her death—
probably after, judging from the look on my face, 1969.

45

husband number two, was crazy about my mother and she was fond of him.

She was an unselfish woman, a so much better person than her daughter. I am not proud of that side of me. I am disappointed and forever saddened by my daughterly lacks. Much of the time I was not worthy of her, but I loved her. She was unquestionably the single most important influence on my life. And how my love for her has grown, more than twenty years after her death! And how much better I am and try to be because of her! Why does it take so long, why does it take a disaster to make you realize what you had? Will it always be that way? Is that human nature?

I thought that dependence on my children would never happen to me. How could it? After all, I am a working woman. I do many things: I am an actress, I lecture, I write, I travel, I have a multitude of interests. I am an independent woman. No, I will never be dependent on my children.

So imagine my shock when I realized, at the tender age of sixty-five, that with all of the above, the final truth is this: I live alone. I need a reason for all that I do, not just to fill my days but to unleash my energy, to make me feel warm, that I matter, to satisfy my emotions. When I travel, which is often, who do I buy things for? My children. To whom do I send postcards? My children. Who do I call? My children. They are my connection. My connection with yesterday, today, and tomorrow. I need them. The truth is out: I depend on them so much more than I told myself I ever would. I can be away from them physically for a while, but I have to talk to them. To know what they're doing, how they are. I am my mother's daughter.

At the end of a working day, at home on a night in (I enjoy my nights in; I enjoy the quiet and the aimlessness of them), I often find myself wondering, what is Steve doing, how is he? And Sam, what's he up to? And Leslie—will she even be there if I call? I'd love to talk to them. I must call them. But then I stop myself. Wait a minute, Steve is with his family, Barbara and Richard and Brooke.

He's got his own life. And Sam has his. Leslie hers. I mustn't invade their time. I mustn't call them too often. I don't want to become an annoyance. Thank God for my beautiful daughter. She has far surpassed her brothers in the phone-call department. Girls often do.

I travel alone—a state I have a love/hate relationship with. For the last twenty-plus years, I have more often than not traveled by myself. I have felt every emotion about it with each trip I have taken—whether Paris, London, Bangkok, or inside the United States. I have hated having to carry my hand luggage, which as I put less and less in it seems to grow heavier each year—don't ask me to explain. Walking into waiting rooms filled with travelers chatting together, I have often felt somewhat uncomfortable sitting alone, being stared at. Yet I've also felt relieved that I could read my book, doze, not have to carry on a conversation from takeoff to landing. I'm getting better at it. I've learned to bury my head in my book on fastening my seat belt, to kill any possibility of the person next to me attempting to start a conversation. Yet at the same time I've wished that I had someone I could talk to. After never in my life having had the courage to sit alone in a drugstore, I now find myself, amazingly enough, actually enjoying solitary travel—for the most part. Having lived on my own for so long, I'm spoiled, I've gotten used to pleasing myself. A dangerous habit, but one I've become rather fond of. Because my work life involves being with many people, I treasure the time that I can go where and when the spirit moves me, without answering to anyone. I am possessed by a restless nature. The day I am housebound will be a sorry day for me.

And I think I have finally figured out that the reason I have always felt awkward being alone in a public place, aside from my natural insecurity (which, despite pigeonholes, still exists), is the perception from my childhood that a woman must have an escort, must be with a man, or people will regard her strangely. Having to travel

This is a ten-year-old photograph of my three special people: they're even better looking today, but I cannot seem to get them in the same place at the same time to repeat the experience, 1984.

alone has forced me to deal with this old-fashioned brainwashing concept. It's only when I think of going to India, Japan, Tahiti, that I blanch at the thought of going alone. (If I had friends there, the problems would be almost nonexistent.) I tell myself, One of these days it will all come together, and I'll go. Then I think, Wait a minute, old girl, one of these days had better come along while you still have the enthusiasm and the interest, not to mention the mobility.

Long trips take it out of you, but I expect and intend to have at least ten to fifteen years of travel capability ahead. I travel well, jet lag not totally but almost wrecking me. It's my stomach that won't adjust. I start off great, then suddenly—upside down, inside out! Even so, it's always worth it. Seeing new places, new faces, hearing new sounds, wakes me up, makes me feel alive, makes me realize how quickly we forget that there's a great big world out there waiting to be explored, that there's more than our own small space, that beyond the blue horizon lie excitement, freshness, discovery, new people, new languages, new cultures—the unknown.

I have a few friends twenty years my senior who still want to see every country on earth—a fabulous attitude, but doesn't a tiny corner of the brain ask, Why? You can't live forever: what about staying in one place and living the rich, full life there? Do you want to spend so much of the rest of your life packing and unpacking, going to and from airports? Sure you do: pack and unpack, go to hotels, see what it's all about, keep the juices flowing—you'll prolong your life. All this may sound a bit restless. Perhaps it is. Routine is not my thing. Though I love my house—the familiarity that resides there—I love it all the more because I cannot be in it on a regular basis. Maybe you never think about the rest of your life in your twenties and thirties or even your forties—I didn't start thinking about the rest of mine until one Sunday in the country. I was sitting on the chaise with Blenheim and found myself thinking: What am I doing here? Why do I hurry out here for the weekend? Who cares that I'm here? This is ridiculous. Where would I really like to be? The answer to that is: I don't know. Everywhere: Paris mostly—London—California—Venice—New

York. Where I don't want to be is in the same place, staring at the same four walls for too long. Or in the middle of a completely set routine: five days in the city, two in the country. Not for me. So no wonder those friends want to keep moving.

One evening several months ago, I returned home from an event I had been dreading. It was the big evening of the Council of Fashion Designers of America —their Academy Awards. They were honoring Oscar de la Renta for his lifetime achievement in design, and rewarding others for their achievements in other branches of the design world. Special tribute was being paid to Diana Vreeland and Giorgio Sant'Angelo, both gone from this world in 1989. I was part of the tribute to Diana Vreeland, that remarkable woman who had been an extremely pivotal figure in my life. She had a great deal to do with the turn that led me to Howard Hawks, Hollywood, and Humphrey Bogart. We had a built-in friendship—not always close, owing to work and life, but persistent because of our connection's early start.

I delivered a short speech about how we had met and what she meant to me, and found myself being looked at and listened to by the major figures of the American fashion world, plus the other presenters. And I was just as frightened then as I was at age seventeen when I first met Diana Vreeland and posed for *Harper's Bazaar*.

When I finally returned home, just before midnight, I took off my beautiful Armani gown, sat down on my bed, and flicked on my answering machine. What should I hear but the voice of my son Steve. I'd been out of town for a week, hadn't had a chance to call him the few days I'd been back, so he called me. What a treat! I was thrilled—and he had left a fairly lengthy message. Did I have a good time in Los Angeles, was I out for dinner or what, and where? I'd have to come home sometime, so please call. I cannot tell you how hearing his voice, his concern, his good humor, made me feel. I wanted him right there so I could give him a great big hug. Then I got to thinking again how little I see of him. My travel in the U.S. usually takes me west, not south, where he was at the time, but I missed seeing him so much, and hearing him made me miss him more.

And I thought about Leslie, out west, far away in miles and time zones. I don't see enough of her either. It's either too late for her to call me when her day ends or too early for me to call her when mine does. I miss her, miss our lengthy conversations. I miss being able to share time. Our approach to life is so different, and she's so different from her brothers—it's good for me to listen to her, hear her point of view. She has expanded my horizons, she is my most natural resource.

Imagine if I hadn't had children. What a horrible thought! What on earth would I have done? How would I have managed my life? These three different beings brought into this world by me, who have given me so much—some pain, some angst, but so much more joy and love. And more than that—a connection with the future.

L ife's abrupt change began with Steve. The shrinking of the only family I had left. He had been going to Boston University. He met a girl—Miss Right! He was twenty; she was nineteen. They were in love; they wanted to get married. They would be engaged first, as I was headed for Europe, taking Leslie, sixteen, and Sam, seven, with me. It would be my last bit of freedom for some time—when I returned to New York I would go into rehearsal for my first musical, *Applause*. The year was 1969. My mother had made too many trips to the hospital that year with her failing heart, but she wanted me to go, wanted life to go on as usual. Like Bogie, she didn't really talk about the dark possibilities, and I realize now that I was afraid to ask. And as with Bogie, I thought the pattern of hospitals would continue. I had no thought of an ending.

Steve had spent a good deal of time away from home from

the age of fourteen, when he had gone to Milton Academy. But he was always home for holidays. He had his room, with all his things always waiting for him. My firstborn, my much-loved, much-pained son, struggling to find an identity of his own while fighting not to be swept away in the undertow of the all-powerful, ever-present overwhelming identity of his father. He looks so like him. How many times had that question been asked: "Are you really Humphrey Bogart's son? What was he really like?" Steve, filled with so many conflicting emotions: resentment, confusion, anger at Bogie for leaving, wanting him there, wanting to know him, wanting to forget the pain of his loss, struggling under the burden of it all, hoping to find someone who would want to be with him for his own sake.

I'm sure he felt marriage was the answer: marriage would give him stability, a position as head of a household, responsibility. He was a young man in need, had been for many years. But he was only twenty—a baby. How could he think that marriage was the answer? I had just broken up with Jason. Steve was too young to know that marriage was tough, took work and thought. Yet he was old enough and stubborn enough to insist on going ahead with it. "*You* did it!" he said. Ah, yes—but under slightly different circumstances. I was more adult, had been out in the world working, and the man I married was a stable, grown-up man. But Steve was his father's son. He had made up his mind, there was no changing it, and he found a way, for himself at least, to be right. Again like his father—who all too often was.

On August 30 of that same year, 1969, I was dealt the devastating blow of my mother's death. That ending threatened for so long had finally become a reality. Steve, who had been living in Connecticut with his bride-to-be, was very attached to his granny, as were Leslie and Sam. I was grateful he was with someone he loved, so he could share his grief. They came to New York for the funeral: it was my first meeting with my future daughter-in-law. Needless to say, I was in no condition to deal with the newness of that—to have any clear picture of them as a couple. My focus was on my mother and the terrible pain I was in.

Steve and I arriving for the dedication of Lincoln Theatre
at the University of Hartford, 1978.

This picture was taken at the end of 1955.

The wedding was to take place in October, before I went into rehearsal with *Applause*. Steve did a terrific and surprising thing: he asked my stepfather, Lee, to be his best man. Lee had been the one continuing male presence in Steve's life—in Leslie's too, for that matter. And he was quite lost without my mother. They had had a really loving and close twenty-one-year marriage. She had given him her family, so in his eyes I was almost his daughter, my children his grandchildren. He badly needed that sense of belonging, being part of us. Steve's special and important request reinforced that sense. Steve's other family members present would be me, Leslie, and Sam; his bride had her parents, her brother, and some friends, if I remember correctly. The wedding was small. The place, his bride Dale's home-town in Connecticut.

I didn't react in any particular way at the time. I accepted it, the fact of it; I had to, and I hoped they'd be happy. After twelve years I thought I'd gotten used to being without Bogie, but the sight of Steve standing there repeating the marriage vows jolted me.

Now, twenty-odd years later, I think of the incredible number of traumatic experiences Steve had undergone during the first years of his life—the death of his nurse while holding him, age two and a half; the death, when he was eight, of his father; the move to England, age nine—new school; the move to New York, age ten—another new school; the death of Mae, our cook, friend, everything, all his life, age twelve. So many burdens, so much constant adjusting—no wonder he was looking for stability, a sense of permanence.

There he was trying to look like a grown-up—trying not to look like the kid he was—and with no father there to give him a boost. And with no husband to give me one, I started to unravel. Also no mother of mine, granny of his, who had always been his champion and a great source of strength and support from the day Bogie died. Oh, how she would have loved to be there, and how terribly badly I needed her to be there. There were so few of us—such a small family. The two people who saved me that day were Leslie and Sam, the fact of them. I thanked God that I had them around me, had them to love, to look after, to share my days with, to come home to. They were my anchors. The fact of being alone was less glaring. Even though for quite a few years Steve had had one foot out the door, not until I saw him drive away toward his honeymoon did I realize that he would be gone from that moment on. That it would never be the same again. It never is. I'd be his mother, he'd be my son, but he had gone from the nest and would never return. That's right, that's as it should be; God knows I did it. Did my mother feel as alone as I did now? She must have, even more so: she had no Leslie, no Sam, to help fill the gap. When we returned home and I walked into Steve's empty room, I realized fully he would never be in that room again, not him alone; that I would never again have first dibs on his time; that he had moved to another place in his life. It's taken me such a long time to understand the parallel of my mother's feelings and fears when I left to marry Bogie. What she must have felt when the daughter she had lived for, worked for, done everything for, would not be around, would not need her in the same way. Why didn't I think of that then? But I would always need her—did she know that? Will my children always need me? I don't know.

I would never fit the grandmother mold. But I went to Steve and Dale when I could, and they came to me when they could. Once their son, Jamie, was born, it became somewhat more difficult, but we tried hard. We did our best. I would bring Sam with me so he would not lose contact with his big brother. As his father and I had split up, I wanted Sam to be with males as much as possible, and big brother was a natural. Now I ask myself: why more with males? Was I thinking they could do so much better than females could—than I could? Would they be more responsible? Not a chance. But that's what programming can do.

Every Christmas I do much the same thing: buy a beautiful Christmas tree, decorate it with every light, every ornament I have meticulously saved over the years, including those kindergarten specials made by each child; creating tradition—family history again. Then, as if to make up for being the only parent around, I buy endless gifts of all sizes, surround the base of the tree with them, hang stockings on the fireplace, fill them to the brim, all to give the feeling that there is more than just me, that there is a well-established family. The reality is that I do it as much to convince myself as to convince the children. I leave out nothing. I buy special candles. I plan a large turkey dinner, with everyone's favorite dish. I take out of the cupboards special objects that I have saved over the years and that I cherish—like the Mexican tree-of-life candelabra Spencer Tracy gave me one year. I think of Spencer often, anyway, but when I have that tree of life prominently displayed, he might almost be there.

I still keep a huge antique Bible that my mother bought at auction after my marriage to Bogie—another reinforcement of family solidarity, security. It doesn't take a psychiatrist to figure out that most of these activities, these feelings, stem from having grown up with one parent, having been abandoned by the other. It so happens that I was lucky: the one parent was a great parent, and she had a great brother, who acted as my surrogate father. I think I've been a pretty good parent, but try as I might, I can never make up for the fact that I am just that—*one*. Single O. I am not a pair. I have no brother, I have no sister, I am not a family. I am not enough. But I stumbled and fumbled my way through those many years, and I still do now, trying to help my children feel there was more. I never quite convinced myself. Why did I think I could convince them? The task was impossible, and I have to admit at this late date in the age of equal rights for women—the great feminist movement—that with children in particular, it is a definite advantage to have a man around the house.

I can't for the life of me figure out why I thought it was more important for Steve to have a male model than for Leslie, but I did. Stupid! But that's a given in early education: boys need fathers more than girls do. Why? Because they are male? Wrong. I know I grew up without mine. Lousy person though he was, he was the only father I would ever have. Though my Uncle Charlie was one of the best men I have ever known and helped me more than any other man until Bogie, he was still my uncle. Corny though it may sound, I could not call him Father. And I am certain that that vacuum has to a great degree colored my behavior with and attitude toward men. Leslie was no different. (She has always referred to Bogie as "Father" —not Dad, not Daddy, but Father, just as he used to call his father.) Though she had the peculiar advantage of growing up with her father on celluloid, she cannot remember his touch. Adding to that the complexities of mother-daughter relationships, and my omissions and errors during her early years, it's a wonder we've done as well as we have together.

Leslie is an unusual young woman, very smart, beautiful, a wry wit, generous of spirit, and very independent. I remember complaining to her once that she had gone too far. Her reply: "But, Mummy, you brought us up to be independent." "I know," said I, "but there's a limit." There is no way to define being independent. You are or you aren't, though there are degrees. I forgot all that when I was bringing up my three offspring. I also forgot that they lived with my example—an independent woman, on the move, self-supporting, alone. With that exposure, how could they be otherwise?

I sent Leslie to the Lycée Français through high school, thinking that with my work taking me all over the world, and the Lycée curriculum the same in all countries, if I took her with me she would have no adjustment to make. Stupid of me, now that I look at it in hindsight. Yet it can't be bad that she can read, write, and speak French. It's what I always wanted for myself. A prime example of my giving her what I wanted—not necessarily what she did. She balked, though, when college time came around. "I'm an American girl. I want to go to an American school." Fair enough. She needed to belong to more than me, Steve, and Sam. She wanted to study art, drawing (Bogie's mother, whom she never knew—nor did I—was an artist). She studied in Boston, and having spent a good deal of time there—art school lasted a year; after that there was college for another year—had the good sense to buy a small house. I was on Broadway

This is a year-old picture of Leslie, the way she looks now,
beautiful, happy, 1993.

with *Applause* for a year and a half, toured for another year, and played in London for yet another year. Boston turned out to be a good move for her. I was busy working. Sam was still small and at home and becoming more and more the center of my life. So Leslie's move away from home did not seem so traumatic at the time. Hell, I had wanted my independence at fifteen, so in actual fact she was two years behind me. And she had a good deal of discovering to do about herself and what she wanted to do with her life.

I won't pretend I always understood her goals, her needs. She did her best to enlighten me, but it didn't always work. She tried many things, each one a learning experience, until she finally found her way to nursing. That meant going back to school, of course, but it was well worth it. Was it genes? Bogie's father was a doctor. Did she have only his genes? Where were mine?

The mother-daughter relationship is about as complicated as it gets. Here we are—two females, loving each other, fighting for our own identities, struggling for understanding. I know; I went through it with my mother. I need to be understood as much in motherhood as I ever did in daughterdom. No one wants to do it badly. We all want the best for our young. We spend much time trying to tell our daughters—our sons—how to live, while telling ourselves we are not interfering. In fact, often it is not interfering; it is informing. The lessons of life are to be passed on—if not parent to child, then to whom? I would tell Leslie about my experiences—what the pitfalls might be, what to avoid—hoping to point the way. What else can we do? I have always fancied myself to be a pretty modern mother. I've worked all my life. My values are well defined and pretty straight. I have been tolerant and impatient simultaneously. Well, I may have been modern to me, but not to her. A generation separated us. So as much as I thought I could see and understand from Leslie's point of view, it was only from the vantage point of what I thought her point of view was, and how, finally, could I know?

We talked—we always talked: thank goodness for that. We still have lengthy conversations, on the phone in particular. Of course,

This was taken on Leslie's birthday on the lawn of our beautiful house, 1954.

Leslie never totally confided in me. Normal. During her quest for a firm, solid place for herself, she would often write me lengthy letters, wonderful letters, explaining her choices, what she was after, pleading for understanding. I did understand intellectually, but not always emotionally. I wanted her to have a life, stay with something long enough to feel secure in work and in herself. I wanted to teach her in much the same way that Bogie had taught me. Why didn't I see the me in her, the me that felt alone and partially abandoned, with no father, and that would probably never feel totally secure? Parents and teachers teach us the definition of a family. A family, they tell us, is a father—head of house, a mother, and a child or children. Does that mean that just a mother or just a father does not a family make? That for a family to be complete, all the elements must be present? No wonder we are confused, unsure, insecure. Why must the rules be so rigid?

Not one of my children has grown up in the accepted American family structure. But then neither did I. I grew up with a single working mother. She was way, way ahead of her time. And so mine have grown up in much the same way. In spite of that, they are —each of them—good people; terrific people, I might say; each with a hang-up or two, but who hasn't who is worthwhile? And all are well-functioning members of this imperfect society in which we live. As is their mother.

Leslie found her way through people—through helping people. At most of the stages in this struggle, we talked. She loved plants, animals, the country, not too much clutter—and everything natural. She has helped me. I have always had a need to talk to her, have always been able to pretty much discuss my personal life with her. She is someone I trust, and she has the patience to listen. I haven't weighed her down with my life problems—that's not my style —but I have been able to unload more with her than with Steve or Sam. Not surprising, I guess: the difference in gender must create an automatic barrier. When Leslie left Boston for California, I knew I would see more of her by virtue of my work. I lived in London for two years, playing *Applause* on the stage and *Murder on the Orient Express* on the screen, and invited Leslie to come over for a couple of weeks. Sam was with me then and was going to the American School. We missed her. Our need for each other became stronger through that period. But Leslie was going to college for her nursing degree and did not want to interrupt that education. Somewhere along the way, she wisely decided that nothing would cut into what she was trying to do with her life. She has never, would never, take time off for travel. If she planned a trip, that was one thing, but she would not accept my offerings. She wanted to be her own person. Well, so she was and so she is.

She has very much her own life now—a definite direction —but with all her independence, we still have our talks. It *is* true what they say: you lose your sons to their wives' families, but your daughters stay with you. The female connection.

As I think about children and parents, it seems to me that the general attitude of children is: "Well, you've lived your life, you've made your choices; now it's my turn. But don't you dare go away." Be there—just in case! Most children seem simply to assume that once they're more or less grown up, that's it! They're off doing their own thing. I was, so I shouldn't be too surprised. Parents are tucked away. Taken for granted. That's the reality. I wonder how aware children are of their parents' needs. How aware was I of my mother's needs? Perhaps a little, but not enough to give up pursuing my own selfish desires. Do my children ever wonder what it's like in my house from the time I wake up to day's end? Do they wonder how I feel? what I eat? whom I see? Did I ever wonder what *her* days were and how she filled them? Her feelings? I knew them, I suppose, but did I really think about them? If pressed, my children say they do about me. But do they really? Do children ever regard a parent as a person: in my case, as a woman, and as a woman who is alone a good deal—by choice partly, but nevertheless alone? Do they realize how little they know us? Did I know my mother? For the most part, I think I did— but did I know her enough? Of course not! I was too involved with my own life.

Let's face it: parents and children adore each other and drive each other crazy from time to time. My wish for my children is that they will always keep their senses and their minds nourished, and that love will remain of paramount importance to each of them.

Seven years ago, after an unpleasant divorce, Steve was introduced to a great girl by his brother Sam, no less. Steve and I had gone downtown to see Sam in a play, then went for supper with Sam and his friend Barbara. A lovely looking girl who suddenly one day many months later was engaged to my son—not Sam, but Steve. All Steve had ever said to me was "I like Barbara—I really like Barbara." And so they were wed and have two beautiful children, Richard and Brooke, and they love each other. Steve is happy, truly happy at last. Barbara puts family first, is terrific with her children, yet remains an independent thinker. He is a good, loyal husband and a wonderful father. Amazing? Not really. He's grown up—not in years, but in himself. With me, of course, he becomes, in spite of his denials, eight years old. Okay, Steve—not always, but from time to time. And there's nothing wrong with that. I was a child with my mother and to her—so you are to me, as is Leslie, as is Sam. Though, luckily for us all, not all the time!

Both Steve and Sam have protested to me that I do not recognize the fact that they are grown men who work, have their own lives, and are responsible adults. Not my little boys. But of course I know they are grown men. I respect their years and how they have filled them; I recognize their adulthood. But you must know, boys, that you will always be my children. When I am ninety and you sixty, you will still be my boys. And it pleases me—so humor me.

They think I expect too much of them. Have they any idea how much they expected, and do expect, from me? And was I the same? Probably not far off. Here's the pattern we're brought up to follow: You grow up, get married, have children, take care of the feeding, clothing, loving of them, send them off to their marriages, to child raising, you become a grandmother and baby-sit for them. It's better now, but the original vision still seems to hang in there. I will not conform. I cannot.

Leslie now has a life to share; that is her first priority. I have a life to live. I guess that is mine.

But I want to see it all. I want to see Steve's Jamie and Richard and Brooke grow up. I want to get to know them. I want the same of Sam's Jasper—I want to give something of me to all of them.

And of course I hope Leslie will have a child. Why? Because I know she'd be a great mother—because I think it's a fulfilling experience—because I think it's necessary to complete the circle of a life. But what Leslie thinks, only she knows, and it's what she thinks that counts.

I couldn't believe it. The voice on the other end of the phone said: "Are you ready to be a grandma again?" Sam, it was Sam, my baby, telling me he and Suzy were going to have a baby. It was unreal. How did it happen so fast, his growing up? There had been small, imperceptible changes since his wedding almost five years before. At times when he's been frustrated in his work and I've told him what to do about it or what I thought he should do, he has said, in the gentlest, nicest kind of way, "You have your way of dealing with things and that's fine for you, and I have mine. I'll handle it, but in my own way." He has taken charge, he is his own man. When I have been angered about something his father did not do and, knowing Sam had been hurt, have made a derogatory remark, Sam still stops me, always says, "Mom, I wouldn't let him talk that way about you, so please don't talk that way about him." Of course he's right, and I so respect and admire how he deals with his life. It all adds up to his knowing who he is, having his own standards and that rare commodity, great character. He knows what his priorities are. I marvel at his clarity.

Sadly, Sam's marriage to Suzy has unraveled. But I can't
—and don't want to—forget how happy it once was, and how happy
I was about it. I remember how all through her pregnancy, Suzy kept
me informed of her progress, sent pictures of her stomach, month by
month. I felt about her the way her mother felt about Sam. It was to
be a natural birth, what they both wanted, and Sam wanted to be part
of every step. I remember their coming to my hotel one night, Suzy
on the floor with Sam massaging her feet, knowing pressure points, as
she practiced her breathing.

I was in the south of France, making a movie, reading in
bed at the end of a working day, when the phone rang. "It's a boy—
eight pounds, fifteen ounces—name of Jasper. [Pause] I cut the cord."
"Hooray! How great! How's Suzy? [Pause] You cut the cord?" Then
came a full description of the birth. On the phone the following day,
Suzy gave me every detail. "I couldn't have done it without Sam." It
was thrilling to hear two people so completely a part of each other. I
was in awe of them. Also more than a little jealous.

As it happened, I was coming to L.A. in two weeks to be in
Rob Reiner's movie *Misery*. Not a large part by any means, but I was
anxious to work with him. The night of my arrival, Sam, Suzy, and
Jasper would come to the hotel for dinner. I was breathless with excitement when the knock was heard. I rushed to open the door, and there,
smack dab in the middle of the hall, was this tiny creature, asleep in a
tiny basket, not a sign of Sam and Suzy, who were hiding off to one
side. It's a funny sight, a tiny baby on the floor, with no one on either
side of him. Only Sam could have thought of that. Two weeks old,
and Sam had been giving him his daily bath. He'd done everything
but nurse him. It was so fabulous to see my baby swinging *his* baby in
his car seat, handling him with total ease. One night he was holding
him, studying him and shaking his head from side to side. I asked him
what he was thinking, and he said, "I just can't believe it." Nor could
I. This child of mine, whom I'd spent so much time with alone,
watching him from year to year: there I was watching him again, as
he held a baby straight out in front of him in his two hands, only it
was not *a* baby—it was *his* baby.

*Applause:* opening night in London with Sam, who has just bowed and shaken hands with Princess Margaret. The year, 1973. Sam, age eleven, on the way to twelve.

. . .

When Sam and I returned from living in London, I often found myself taking him with me, whether visiting friends or dining with them, as long as it didn't interfere with his school life. My friends welcomed him; he made them laugh. That is one of his greatest gifts. And I am a sucker for anyone who makes me laugh. I prize humor more highly than most other attributes. I certainly could never have made it through my life's miseries without it. I found that I enjoyed being with Sam more than with most people. After two years in England, the shock of reentry into New York was monumental. I felt so uprooted, so displaced, alien—as did he. But we had each other, that was a constant, and I suppose we clung to that more than we should have. Certainly I did.

My friends were still my friends, but their lives had gone on without me for two years. It isn't easy for me to face the fact that other people, even my friends, are much more interested in their own lives than they are in mine. Ridiculous—of course they are! Why wouldn't they be? Clearly I expect or need too much, or both. As long as I had Sam at home, I had a life to share in a way—at least someone to wake up for, to do things for, to laugh with. I'd had him nine years after Leslie, and my pattern had remained unbroken. I was the head of my household, the *sole* head, for most of my adult life. I could make the rules, keep a home going and together, and for the most part not feel the need to have a constant significant other. Though many's the time I wished I had one.

As Sam started to grow up, and as New York had become more of a jungle in our absence and he was too old for a nanny, I felt he would be safer and happier with boys his own age, in a male-accented atmosphere. There goes that programming again, or brainwashing if you will. Besides, I knew I would have no one to leave him with when called to whatever location to work. For the work must go on, and the incidents of danger on his way home from school had become all too frequent. So after much thought, much discussion, and much pulling of my strained gut and torn heart, Sam and I started to look for boarding schools. Steve had gone to boarding school, and Sam knew how much he had enjoyed the experience, so he accepted it. But it was terribly hard for him, much harder and more painful than I realized until some years later.

The process takes doing. I had forgotten what I went through with Steve, writing for brochures to five or six schools, sending school records to them, making appointments with headmasters, then traveling to a different school every weekend for an interview. And after all that, waiting for the letter of acceptance. And after all *that*, the decision: which one was best, which one did Sam prefer. Finally a decision was made: Salisbury School, in Connecticut, had won the day. A beautiful campus, a first-class curriculum, a not too highly pressured atmosphere, a very sympathetic headmaster, lovely houses all around the grounds. It was far and away the most appealing of all the schools. Sam said he felt comfortable there; I was comfortable for him. Jason lived not far away, as did Steve, so there would always be a family member in easy reach; Sam would feel more secure, less isolated. This, of course, was me reassuring myself and deciding what Sam's feelings would be—never stopping to take a good look, to examine the reality, the possibility that I might be making a mistake. Yet I saw no other way. I had to work, and I hadn't a clue what or where that work might be. I don't think I ever really analyzed how I would feel without Sam at home. I know that I never felt that I, alone, was enough for him. I knew I had to work for my own sake or I would have no purpose in my life, and I had to make a living. And so we started buying the necessities and the personal decorations for his new adventure.

I will never forget that heartbreaking first day of taking Sam to school. We drove up—Blenheim, Sam, and I. We met the headmaster, who was receiving the parents and the new students, welcoming us. We were introduced to Sam's housemaster, taken to the house that would be his home for a year, to the room he would share with another new boy. At the main house, where tea was being served, parents began to leave. The headmaster had told me it would be best if I didn't hang around for too long, better if I just left Sam there and let him fall into the ways of the school and the other boys. Trying to be unobtrusive, I kept one eye on Sam, to see how he was doing. The leave-taking was torture. He looked so small—so much smaller and younger than he was; he looked so forlorn, so lost, so brave. I could almost physically feel that imperceptible rupture of the umbilical cord. It took every ounce of control not to pick him up and take him right back home with me, not to burst into tears. I told him to call me anytime he wanted, and I would call him. I would visit him, of course, every Sunday that I was in town, not working. I would take him to Steve's for the weekend. His father would visit him. He just nodded; said little, just looked at me. It broke my heart. As I remembered, or tried to, those many years before, it had not been the same with Steve. He was much more prepared to go away to school, even looked forward to it. Hmm, I think now, did he want to get away from me? Or did he just want to be with other boys, doing boy things, without reporting to Mother? I have no answers.

It was so strange to walk into my apartment with no Sam there. All those quiet, empty rooms seemed suddenly alien, cold, unfriendly. Only gradually, over time, did I become aware that from the age of twenty-four I had always lived with a child, and with the exception of a few months at the start of my contract with Howard Hawks, I'd never lived alone. Startling in retrospect: married at twenty, had lived with mother, grandmother, and uncle all the years before, and ever after with children and, for a while, with husbands.

Suddenly four years had gone by, and Sam was graduating from Salisbury, thinking of college and becoming an actor. One year of college led to the pursuit of an acting career. He was making his own choices for his own life. Salisbury had turned out to be the right choice, a happy experience for him. Our closeness never abated, but as he grew into young manhood his interests spread out and the search

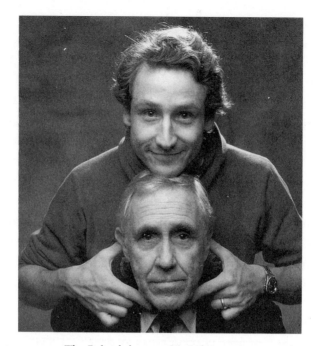

The Robards boys, 1986, *Life* magazine.

for his niche on the planet became of primary importance. And why
not? It was completely natural, to be expected. Hadn't I done it? How
quickly I had forgotten my own drive to get out in the world, be
independent, on my own, make my mark in the theater—make my
fantasy a reality. I had a burning, passionate ambition. My mother
had been totally supportive, no questions asked. I was supportive of
Sam, but of course felt obliged to warn him of the pitfalls, the life of
rejection and anxiety that was the core of every actor's life.

Bogie had always been proud of being an actor: thought it
a noble profession and that actors, real actors, were to be admired. But
it is a tough profession, and if it doesn't mean everything to you, if
you might be content doing something else, by all means do something else; you'll save yourself a lot of heartache. I felt that same way,
and I passed it along to Sam. Jason is an actor—a brilliant actor—and
he told Sam the same thing. Parents are forever trying to protect their

children from the danger and misery that is lurking out there. Children are forever champing at the bit to get out there and find out for themselves. Anyway, Sam had made his choice: an actor he would be. And an actor he is, and a damn good one, I'm happy and relieved to say. I say relieved, because supposing he hadn't been good? How horrible it would be to have a child with no talent for his chosen profession and horrible to have to face that fact. How does one deal with that? I suppose there is a way, but I'm grateful I'll never have to find it.

Though Sam had been away at school, spent nights away with friends, he was to all intents and purposes, and as far as I was concerned, living at home. His room was still his room, still filled with his things, kept as he wanted it kept. I always had food for him, special things that he liked. The Zabar's fix has always been part of my children's lives—particularly Leslie's and Sam's. Steve was never crazy about the Sunday fare that in my house consists mainly of Nova Scotia salmon, sliced paper thin, center cut so it's not too oily; cream cheese with scallions, smoked whitefish, half-sour pickles; bagels of the garlic, poppy, and sesame seed variety. When Leslie comes to town I stock up, and all through Sam's life in New York I've gotten these foods for him. Some of this is a hangover from my childhood days. Delicatessen food has been part of my life for as long as I can remember. There has never been a taste quite as good as a hot pastrami sandwich on rye bread with coleslaw. Also it's the Jewish mother in me: genetic, I suspect. Food is basic and another way to connect with your children—to please them, to build tradition. I do believe that when my children come to visit, they expect the food that they get only at my house—that isn't a staple at theirs. Is that a way of hanging on to childhood? Theirs or mine? I wonder.

Sam came to London for my opening in Tennessee Williams's *Sweet Bird of Youth* at the Haymarket Theatre. A few days after that, as we were sitting at breakfast, he said he had something to tell me. Any parent begins to quake when hearing that. I took a deep breath, expecting I don't know what, and then he broke it to me: "I've asked Suzy to marry me." He was nervous, actually apprehensive, not sure what my reaction would be. He was so anxious that I love her as he did. Well, I did. It was a great moment for me; Sam was so touching, so moving. I looked at him and realized that all these months he had been falling in love with this girl and thinking seriously about making his own life as a young man. And at twenty-three, he was sure of his choices, sure of his decisions. It had not occurred to me that he might be thinking of marriage. He stayed in London for about two weeks and was on the phone at least once a day with Suzy. I would hear him talk to her—what he felt, how he felt, so completely vulnerable. He planned to go to Oklahoma to formally ask Mr. Amis —Suzy's father—for her hand. And he was very nervous at the prospect. I was charmed and taken completely by surprise, by Sam's really proper, traditional, and almost old-fashioned approach to this marriage. I thought of myself when I first fell in love with Bogie. He had been the articulate one, the one who could express his feelings easily and poetically. He was so much older, had been through so much. I, on the other hand, was so young, had been through very little, and had never been one to articulate my emotions. I felt them—oh, yes, I most definitely felt them all. I could say I love you and mean it, though they were three words not often spoken in my growing-up years. But to completely bare my soul, as Sam seemed to be doing— no, I do not think I would have been able to do that, nor have I ever. I must make clear that I was brought up by emotional people in an emotional household, but "I love you" was not an everyday phrase. It was just there, that love—just felt. It's a marvelous thing to be able to tell someone exactly what you feel for him or her, not to be afraid of rejection. I'm truly in awe of that vulnerability, that innocence, that trust of another human being, so I suppose I am in awe of my son for the part of him that moves forward, plunges ahead, isn't careful. It's so brave.

And I would say it is most assuredly due to Sam's openness that I almost never end a telephone conversation with Steve and Leslie without saying "I love you" to them, and they in turn are able to respond more than they used to. I think, too, that as you get older, you realize more and more, through the loss of loved ones—family and friends—how filled with regret you are because of what you didn't say. The value of "I love you," of telling people what you feel, how much they mean to you, looms very large indeed. How many times have I wished I could jump back in time so I could say what I never said enough to my mother, to Bogie, to friends: the "if only"s and "I wish"es tumble one on top of the other. I hope Bogie knew how much I loved him, how much he meant to me, how highly I valued him. I told him, but not enough. I hope my mother knew that I admired and adored her, was proud of her. I didn't show her enough. The living are so careless. I was so careless.

I don't want Steve or Leslie or Sam to have those same regrets. I hope Steve tells Barbara how he feels about her. I hope he tells his children all through their growing-up years how much he loves them and has faith in them and is proud of them. Steve covered up so much for so long, had buried so many feelings for so many years, spent his growing-up years not wanting to feel, not wanting to go through the pain again. He was the first child for Bogie—the first for us—and the realization of all I had promised his father from the beginning. I have not articulated all of this to Steve myself, but I hope he somehow gets the message—for he is not a hugger himself. Nor was Bogie. Though Steve used to be, and he's able to do it with a bit more ease now. When he was small, he couldn't hug enough. But early scars run deep, and each of us deals with them in the best way he can, just to get through the days. Not as grim as it sounds: I mean getting through life with as few personal hurdles to jump as possible. We all arrive at adulthood carrying baggage; the aim is not to carry too much.

Leslie, too, went through many years of pain through loss and held it deep inside her—though she did actively try to work it through with help. But shyness and insecurity made her unable to voice her "I love you"s with great ease. Now she finds it more often than not a part of our conversations. They are rewarding, these changes, and luckily we are susceptible to them—luckily they come with years lived.

Even though I had a loving, though lopsided, one-parent childhood, I always dreamed of a sister, a brother, yearned for it as a matter of fact, longed for someone to share with, confide in. I still feel this longing, despite observing the problems some of my friends have had with their siblings: the competitiveness, the demands, the jealousy. But then that can be true about almost any relationship. I am certain, however, that the reason I have been overly possessive of my friends dates back to being an only child and fantasizing my closest friend or friends as surrogate sisters.

It seems that whenever I have been upset or annoyed with Steve or Sam, Leslie's the one I have unloaded on—my bouncing board, my leveler. An awful burden to have placed on her. I apologize to you publicly, my darling daughter. It comes from not having a significant or even an insignificant other to tell my troubles to. These troubles are seldom monumental—never insurmountable—but they are troubles to me. When I argue with my children, it is often because I want them to appreciate what I appreciate, even if it's tables and chairs (that's for Steve, who cares not at all whether it's old or new, as long as it's comfortable). Leslie hears about it, no one else, because I believe family matters should not venture outside the immediate family. That was drummed into me from childhood by my mother, my grandmother: What happens within a family is sacrosanct, must be protected and remain unknown to all outsiders.

When I'm sure I'm right in an argument, my children are reluctant to side with me. While in my eyes it is not a matter of siding but a recognition of where right lies. I would never pit one child against the other; they wouldn't stand for it even if I did. Though they don't verbally side with their siblings, I am certain that is where their sentiments lie. And who can blame them? Yet it infuriates me at times; I still can't believe they don't think as I do about certain life happenings and behavior. Somehow, somehow, no matter how much they love me—which I hope is a lot—I am still that figure of authority, and they stick together. Looking at it as unemotionally as I can (and of course I really can't), I'm glad they do. Through all their early tragedies and traumas of loss, they had each other, and that thread is as strong as iron now and always will be.

I don't take credit for what they have become, but I do believe I have made positive contributions to each of their characters, character being number one on my list of important traits. Now they are gone from my nest to make nests of their own. I have always thought, I was always taught, watch the birds, they make their nests, have their young, feed them, make them strong, and when they are ready to fly, out of the nest they go. I can't speak for the birds, but for myself, I knew they would go. I wanted them to make their own lives, I wanted that, and now they've gone and done it, and I miss them.

Women who have spent the greater part of their adult years raising their children—what do *they* do? They must feel terribly lonely. Thank goodness for today's awareness of women's capabilities and our realization that if we want to, we can do anything and every-thing. That it's our choice. We all have a reason to be; we just have to find it. If you've spent twenty years or more putting your energy and self into raising your children, whatever you wanted to be or thought you wanted to be during the college years has long since faded away. But finally, life cannot be only about submerging yourself to develop others, so that when the others are developed you are finished, have nowhere to go.

Could that have happened to me? Over and over again I tell myself: I will never, could never, be dependent on my children. As long as I am working I am content. But is that really true? I think not. I need more: not a lot more, but more. Am I being greedy? Of course. I love to work, I need to work: to use myself creatively, my brain, my body. But is every day until the end only that? Am I just filling the days? That's like looking for the answer to—the meaning of life. And if the answer to life isn't in your children, if you've been lucky enough to have them, in what is passed onto them, then where is it?

As each birthday of Steve, Leslie, and Sam approaches, I think back to the day they were born, when I gave birth. Where I was, how I lived, who was there—it's all so vivid to me. The growing-up time, though far away now, still evokes pictures of lives lived then, all covering more than forty years. How is it possible? I don't feel old, except sometimes. I don't look old, I don't think. I don't act old, whatever that means—not compared to really old people. That's funny: how old is old? How old is really old? Depends on your vantage point. Old to me is not so much years, anyway, as it is behavior— how you think, walk, talk; energy, interest, enthusiasm, curiosity, awareness. Even to actually realize that my three were born so many years ago is hard. It all still seems new to me, despite what we've all been through separately and together.

Thoughts of one's mortality have a way of creeping into the foreground from time to time after you're sixty. I don't think about it for long or even often, but I do find it suddenly raising its head when I reflect on such possibilities as: should I try to buy a pied-à-terre in Paris, a studio in London, a tiny Spanish house in California. Once I have it I'll have to use it. Will I go there often enough to warrant it? Or at this stage of life is there any point to a heavy investment in anything? Or why am I selling the house I have, only to be saddled with yet another? For the children? No. That's no reason to buy anything. If there is one thing I've come to realize, it's that my children don't want half the silver, tables, chairs, tchotchkes I have. Leslie wants to live without clutter. Steve's location has been somewhat impermanent, though now he's heading for his first home ownership—hooray! And Sam's on the move again; our tastes are very much alike, but he doesn't want to be burdened with too many things. And all three of them naturally want to choose their own things at their own pace, to fill their own needs. They may love what I have, but their lives are different from mine. I filled my house with wonderful furniture and art to satisfy my aesthetic sense and as a way of building a solid life, surrounding myself with antiques, tradition, subconsciously thinking that all that would bring me stability, permanence. Then Bogie died, and I was left with all those tables and chairs, which I wanted no part of at first, which I almost resented for being there when he wasn't, and which now, having seen me through those years, comfort me. But none of my children lives that way or seems to need that tradition, except for Sam, who one day may want to build a home in one place, even though his work might keep him from spending too much time there. The differences among the three of them are of endless fascination to me. Why do they want and don't want the things in life that they want and don't want? Steve has the same pride in ownership of a home that Sam does but feels completely differently about what's inside. Leslie had a house in Boston for more than a decade. It was filled with lovely furniture, but she had it stored for years until she was sure where she was going to live; she just didn't feel strongly about having her own things around her.

Some years ago, when I was playing in *Woman of the Year* on Broadway, before I left for the theater one day I told the children to make a list of the things of mine they really wanted, because I had so much stuff and couldn't figure out how to divide it up in my will. Naturally, they were horrified, but they joked about it. The thought of my demise was something none of them wanted to think about (I didn't want to think about it either), but by God they did it. When I returned from the theater the lists were made. We went over them together amid much guffawing and fooling around, but it helped me. I did say, "Look, I don't intend to leave this world for a hell of a long time, but I need these for my will—then we'll forget about it." They were able to deal with that, they were adorable, they were funny and became children again. I was very moved. It was a rare emotional moment for me, when I could look at all three of them and sense how much they cared for me and for each other.

I think often of what I can give them now. I couldn't care

less about leaving a great legacy behind; I'd much rather have them enjoy it all while I'm around. Suddenly I feel submerged in my possessions, possessed *by* them. I'll try to outsmart my sons and daughter, but it won't be easy. The picture of a mother forcing her belongings on her children would make a great cartoon. Where are you, Charles Addams?

Dividing all this, plus whatever jewelry I have, so that no one will be offended is a nightmare. Definitely a no-win situation. They don't care now, those children of mine, but they will later, and I don't want any of them to harbor any hurt feelings or feel left out or that I was playing favorites. I can only do what I think is right and hope that it is. All this comes of owning too much. Possessions, things, are wonderful to look at, to live with, to adorn oneself with, but they are a pain when disbursement time rolls around. It's too peculiar to be talking, even thinking, about all this, especially in view of the fact that I've still got most of my marbles and I'm still moving around at a pretty good clip, with a fairly youthful, active approach to life. But that's the best time to think about it, when you can joke about it. Dealing with it as I have also makes it seem less serious, less inevitable and definitely much further away. I like that.

Stop for a moment and ponder on the silliness of it. You spend a good part of your adult life acquiring things: building a home, filling it with objects that please your eye and make you feel comfortable. Then you spend the last part of your life trying to figure out how to get rid of it all. Makes no sense, but the only alternative is to have nothing—which would make me feel that I belonged nowhere—or not try to divide the goods, just leave it up to the children, let them figure it out. Now, that is more than anyone should be asked to deal with. Well, *my* children will be old and gray when I depart this earth, for I have every intention of living forever, or as close to that as whoever decides these things allows.

# THE HOUSE

For years some of my best friends had country
houses, to which I was invited from time to
time. Then in the spring of 1970, after the opening of *Applause* on
Broadway, I found myself in the producer-supplied limo every Saturday night, heading for Amagansett, to put my feet up and be cared for
by my dear friend Mary Stone until my departure Monday at noon. I
became a regular tenant, part of the household. Mary would wait up
for me every Saturday night, and while munching on cheese, salami,
bread, we'd catch up on the rest of our lives. Peter and Mary's house
is woody, easy, filled with just enough of everything: feeding the eye
and the stomach; fires roaring; animals everywhere. It was heaven for
me. Mary would appear on Sunday morning with a glass of fresh
orange juice, then proceed to cook bacon and eggs. Peter would go
early for the Sunday paper, getting an extra one for me. He was very
patient; it cannot be great for anyone's privacy to have a friend—the
*same* friend—no matter how close, moving in every weekend. But
they put up with it, and it put no strain on our friendship. It was the
dormitory life I had never had.

The Long Island air as a steady diet is clear, clean, fresh. The ocean on one side, the bay on the other, and in the middle great trees, wonderful old houses, village life—which was always part of my belonging fantasy—and beautiful gardens. In short, it has everything. City cares and pressures fall away. And in fall and winter, when the summer tourists have gone, it is peaceful.

I would bring Sam with me always, except in summer, when he was in camp. Often we would go to Phyllis and Adolph Green's, in East Hampton, where Sam's pals Adam and Amanda resided. The Greens are two of my oldest and most cherished friends, so the attractions were endless.

I became aware of birds and started to single them out and watch them. In that part of the world one can see grackles, blue jays, chickadees, cardinals, all gather together in one afternoon, with squirrels and chipmunks on the sidelines. Walks in the woods, leaves of all colors, dogs—what a picture! I had forgotten how important the country was to me. Through the sixties I had become totally involved in work and my children, and except for work trips to California (which was like a second home to me, after all), Central Park had been my major or, at least, my steadiest respite from cement. Certainly the closest. My apartment overlooks the park. That openness became a fourth wall.

But being the Stones' guest began to get to me: slowly, I admit, but it began to happen. I was out of New York on a national tour of *Applause* for almost a year until the summer of 1972, then I worked in England for two years. They were two years filled with highs and lows. Work highs, personal highs, followed by personal lows. Yet I wouldn't have traded any of it; I only wish the highs had lasted longer. Don't we all? I'm afraid it's not in the grand design.

All through my two years in London, Mary Stone called me weekly. Although I had many friends in England and actually was living across the street from two more of my oldest and dearest, Joan and George Axelrod, and around the corner from two more, Sam and Mildred Jaffe, I was out of touch with many of my friends and, more important, my two older children. Of course, Steve and Leslie were living on their own by that time, but I did miss them terribly, and I called them. Thank heaven for the telephone, the bearer of the worst as well as the best, but a lifeline. The calls from Mary and Peter not only kept me in touch but also helped me to feel remembered. I had been thinking about getting a place of my own out in the Hamptons. I asked Mary to keep her eyes open, as she was out on the Island much of the time and she and Peter really knew the territory.

I couldn't afford anything grand. I didn't want anything that required steady help or had too much cultivated land. When I got back to New York I started to look, but rather casually. I didn't realize then, though I do now, that I had always thought of houses in relation to the way I lived in California when Bogie was alive and times were productive and good. There I very quickly got used to large rooms, dressing rooms, swimming pools, gardens. I forgot that you had to pay for all that—somebody did—and that you had to take care of it. I never bothered to ask how it all got there. I wasn't really thinking practically. I wasn't thinking, period.

I went with Peter to look at a house he had just bought or was about to buy for rental purposes. He had an immediate vision of what to do with it, where to put everything—ceiling beams, pool, etc. He was gifted in the realm of the redoing-of-houses. I hadn't a clue; I had to see more there to begin with. I remember going back to that same house with Peter when it was nearly done, and it was adorable. What a difference!

I looked at one terrific house with Mary: great downstairs living room, but a bad kitchen; work would have to be done. And the thought of it put me off. If I'd known then what I know now. Ah! Experience! We kept looking, and between forays into unknown atmospheres, I cozied up to the safe, warm, comfortable Stone house. A hard place to leave, safety being a rare feeling for me.

I was in California making *The Shootist*—it was near the end of shooting—and one morning the phone in my bungalow rang. It was Mary. A perfect house was coming on the market, and when was I coming home? The minute it was made public it would be snapped up. Well, I was to leave L.A. in two weeks and then leave for London three days after arriving in New York. So we set it up. I'd get out there Saturday night, on Sunday morning we'd go to the house, and I'd return to New York Sunday night. When these things happen, they happen fast. No time to shift your weight from one foot to the other. Mary gave me an entire detailed description of the house and promised to measure the bedrooms and closets. Pictures were sent. She was certain that this was the house for me. "I see you in it," she kept saying. Forget the pea-green living room and the tiny kitchen, the too-small bedrooms; it all can easily be fixed; a great house. And the price was fair and good—that is, fair and good if you could swing it. She had the real estate agent call me. I prevailed on her to wait until I got there and could actually see it, but from the sound of it, it was what I'd been looking for. As she knew me and had shown me other houses and pretty well knew my taste, she agreed with Mary that this one was for me. I immediately phoned my business manager, gave him details, and told him I would gladly sell whatever stock I had for the down payment. It was up to him to figure it out and make it work.

Incredible to even contemplate making a decision like that, of that importance, so quickly. I must have been mad. I've been this kind of mad for a long time.

All went as planned. I arrived home, unpacked, went out to Peter and Mary's the next afternoon. Sunday morning we went to the house, driving up a shortish driveway, with tall pine trees standing majestically on a sloping lawn. The house rested just above, at the edge of the trees. Now, this was December, cold, gray, not the most flattering light for any of us. The house was a nice English-cottage shape; gray wood-shingle roof, up a few steps to the front door, enter, and there was the pea-green living room. Ugh! A nice-sized room with a window seat in a bay window, always a plus. As I toured the rooms, Mary gave a running commentary on easy improvements—a closet here, a door there, move the fridge, paint everything white, always.

There is nothing so cold, so impersonal, so dead as an empty, unlived-in house. As I had almost sealed this deal from California, there was nothing for it but to go all the way. So though it was not absolutely love at first sight, it was enough for an engagement. The right time for me to make this move. I looked at my smiling friends, who were thrilled that I was making a decision and the right one. Mary planned with me what we'd do, room by room. Peter (who I suspect was a bit relieved that I was not to be a permanent fixture in his house, and who could blame him?) told me he'd give me a list of every service person, painter, handyman, house-watcher (never heard of it before —does a person just sit and watch a house? there was no such thing as a house-watcher in all my years of California home owning), garbage pickup, grocery, garden man, pest control, and on and on. It all sounded so simple. They would help me to make it simple. I cannot believe that after the fifteen years I lived in California I still didn't really understand the working of a house, the requirements. Bogie had brought his great cook, gardener, and secretary to our marriage, and his business manager, so I never broke down who did what and how they did it to keep a house going; they were just there; part of our lives. I had more or less, I now realize, played house for all those years. How naive I was to think for a moment that anything to do with home owning was simple.

I was excited at the prospect of living in a house again. The amazing thing to me about California, after having been born and brought up in New York, totally cement-, elevator-, bus-, and subway-oriented, was that I could open my front or back door and walk directly onto a lawn. No city girl could believe it. Plus the fact that I could get into my car and drive to the market or to friends anywhere and then drive back to my own house. What a marvelous feeling that was! And now, here in Amagansett, I would be able to do that again. Sam would love it, Steve and Leslie would have a place to come to in the country when they could (they all hated city life). Blenheim would be happy. A perfect family picture flashed before my eyes. To end that momentous day, we went to Peter and Mary's house to celebrate and then drove back to New York. It was somewhat unreal to me. I had bought a house in almost the same way I would buy a sweater.

And then I was heading for Europe on business. From that trip on, every subsequent visit—to England in particular—would provide some choice table or chair or lamp for my house. I had even decided on a name for the house: SW1. SW1 stands for Southwest 1, the section of London I had lived in for two happy years. In every way possible, my new house would be an extension of my London life, a continuing attachment to it, and, as I think of it now, one of the contributing reasons I would not feel I totally belonged in Amagansett.

On my return to America, the first thing I did was to take Sam, then aged sixteen, to see it—particularly to see his room. The layout of the house was quite ideal: downstairs a combination living-dining room, the pea-green-soon-to-be-white room, the minuscule kitchen; upstairs, two small bedrooms and one really small one; mine had a bath, Sam's a bath next door; and there was an attic with a pull-down ladder. All this part of the original over-hundred-year-old house. The previous owners had added a downstairs guest room and large bath and a great high cathedral-ceilinged all-purpose room, with sliding doors that led to a wooden deck overlooking a small rose garden, trees, and wild growth. The entire property encompassed an acre, but easily half of it was wild. Even the name of my street—Further Lane —was lonely, I thought. Sam thought it was all great, of course.

The decorating began. I love doing that, making a nest. I was lucky too. I had a friend, an antique dealer named Garvin Mecking. I'd known him for more than ten years by that time. He had a great eye, great taste, and, even more special, great wit. He bought all kinds of furniture, mostly English-Welsh-Dutch, and his choices were original, the quality first-rate, the prices fair. His style leaned to the country. I couldn't wait for him to see the house.

I had promised my business manager I would not spend a lot of money on the decor; only necessities at first, all else slowly. Buying the house was a major investment. As 1978 was the last year of my devoting almost all my time to writing my autobiography, I did not have much acting money coming in. Fortunately, I had an overflow of furniture in New York, both in storage and in my apartment. Not as I would like it, but good enough for a start.

I started by measuring walls. I really started by hiring a painter—everything white. (Wallpaper would not be changed yet; one step at a time.) I arranged for him to go in on his own while I was in the city, so by the weekend I was to come out it would be finished. Of course, I had to check up on him to see that it was what I wanted and the way I wanted it. That striving for perfection is the monkey on my back. For as long as I can remember, I have driven people mad pursuing this goal—husbands, children, and myself included. I extend to them all my apologies and my deepest sympathy, but I also figure and hope it's part of my questionable charm.

Finally it was done. What a difference two coats of white paint make! Garvin came out to look it over and immediately saw several things he had in his shop that would work perfectly. From that time on, until the house was finished, I didn't make a move without checking with him.

So it began. Oh, wouldn't this look terrific on that wall? What a marvelous chair! I think one wall would be great with framed needlepoint animals—particularly needlepoint Cavalier King Charles dogs—like the wall I have in New York. The difference in this house will be that almost all adornment, all bibelots, will have to do with nature: birds, animals of all persuasions, wild and indigenous to the area, land and water inhabiting. Once that point was established, there was no holding me. Carved wooden deer heads and entire deer (not live ones), rabbit paintings, pheasant tile tables, sprang up in every corner of the room. All my idea of necessities.

Once again I was building a nest, living a stage set—another fantasy of mine. It made me feel that I had an immediate solid family life. I was going through this process in much the same way that a real couple does. The glaring difference, of course, was that I was not a couple, this was a solo operation. Didn't stop to think about that at the time, that finally it would be just me. After all, I was married at twenty, was immediately thrust into living in a house that I was expected to run, with servants inside and out. Funnily enough, I completely accepted it. It never occurred to me that I'd never had servants, that I'd never lived in a house, that I wouldn't be able to cope. It wasn't confidence: I never have had much of that; it was blind trust. It had been a great adventure, the couple life. From that day in May 1945 when I took my vows, I was committed to being half of a pair—to making a house a home.

So now I jumped in with both feet, and bit by bit, table by table, chair by chair, room by room, my house was created. Every chance I had, I went out there. It was a perfect place to write; I used a temporary dining room table. And it got cozier and cozier. I loved the detailing of the house—the placement of things. The first thing I did in the kitchen, which was truly minuscule, was to have pine shelves put up on all walls. That's where would rest especially handsome pots, baskets, wooden boards. Trays would stand against the wall at the back of the counter. I put everything I could squeeze into that tiny space. Atmosphere.

I loved the house, especially in winter: a lighted fire is always one of the better sights in any room. I forgot that fireplaces must be cleaned. Who, me? I never entertained! Funny, now when I think of it, I entertained so much in California, and enjoyed it. In truth, it was fun, but it was new and I had an organized house and an organized life, and I was half of a pair. Never mind: I do love it when people come to my house.

Sam and I had a great time together, and I took him almost everywhere with me. It was an enormous plus for me; first of all, having a young son made me feel younger, and needed. It also kept that family feeling alive. And I came to depend on him. When Sam was in the country I had someone to fix breakfast for, buy food for, pick up after, even to yell at. There was another sound in the house. Despite the fact that I was driven out of the room because of the television and the hi-fi all going at once, I was happier when he was around. Of course, Sam wanted a pool, though he loved going to the beach. I, too, wanted a pool; swimming is my main sport: I've always loved it, from camp days.

So there I was, thinking about changing, adding. I had been working with a marvelous man, Bill Jones, who knew every tree, flower, shrub, leaf, everything that grows—and ran a great nursery. From day one, one of my greater pleasures was the garden. First to deal with what was there: it had been neglected, I'm sorry to say. Then to start adding. Adding is my specialty. Since that day those many years ago when I began to learn the botanical as well as common names of flowers and trees in California, I have been a garden lover. There is something extremely satisfying in the recognizing and naming of each flower, shrub, and tree that grows on your land. This particular garden was going to be my creation from scratch and without a gardener. (Low maintenance—who was I kidding?) Sometimes my naiveté staggers me, and this would be one of those times. Bill and I started to plan. There was nothing but uncultivated wildness where the swimming pool would go. A few great trees that would remain. After establishing the pool's exact location, I could begin to plan the garden. There would have to be some semblance of a garden if one was to spend time in and around the pool. Did I think what it might cost? Of course not. I also would have to build some kind of small shed to house pool equipment, motors, filters, heaters, and the like. Did I think about that? Absolutely not. A real project was in the making. No sooner had the inside become almost the way I wanted it, at least for the moment, than I had to start on the outside. It must be my restless nature.

I wanted an English garden. On every trip I'd made to England, every weekend at the Sidney Bernsteins' in Kent, Russell Page would either spend the weekend or come for Sunday lunch. A tall, very handsome, and lovely man, Russell was known worldwide as a landscape architect emeritus. He had written what was the textbook for anyone in that field and even for the likes of me. He had great taste, and of course I thought of him as a friend, not realizing at first to what extent he was revered in serious gardening circles. He had been commissioned by the Frick Collection to design its garden area, which stands today as beautiful as ever. His last gigantic undertaking was the Pepsico gardens, in Purchase, New York. Russell knew Long Island well, having done several important Southampton estates, and he understood what would and would not grow there. I told him I liked many different flowering plants, trees, etc., mentioning some specifically, but that I wanted an English garden. He said, "If you want an English garden, plant one of everything that you like, and you will have an English garden." He named some varieties that would thrive in my soil and environment. I dutifully wrote them down and on my return to Amagansett listed them for Bill Jones. The garden grew via Bill, Russell, me, England, and all points east. Even west: remembering those plants I loved in L.A. And when it was finished it was a triumph. It also had to be planned with an eye to maintenance —as little as possible. Ha! Of course, I forgot about my compulsiveness, my extremism, the totally impractical side of me. As the garden began to take shape, Bill and I would walk around it, figuring out what would go where. Waving a hand to the left and right, I would casually mention the ten or twenty flowers, shrubs, trees that I adored, and he'd write them down, eliminating those that had a questionable future in that environment, and proceed to find places for each of them. It never occurred to me that I would have to pay for any of this. I don't understand at all how or why I became so casual about the cost of things. All I can assume is that I only understand saving small sums. I grew up having fifteen-cent lunches. I don't throw away small sums of money, but I have no comprehension of the larger picture; don't talk hundreds and thousands to me—they're just numbers. So whenever over the past twelve years I've done anything to the house, I just waved a hand. And so my garden grew. No silver bells, no cockleshells, no pretty maids all in a row: it just grew. It was exactly what I wanted: azaleas and rhododendrons in the shade to the left of the lawn leading to the pool. A cherry tree with a myrtle ground cover to the right, with a few roses thrown in.

Except for August, the worst month for flowering plants,

there was always something in bloom from March, crocus time, on. And it was forever green. My friends adored it. One summer, my dear friends Tony Walton and Gen Leroy spent August there while I was away working and they were waiting for their house in Sag Harbor to be ready for occupancy. Tony, who is a camera buff, photographed all my flowers one by one and presented this collection to me on my return. A great gift. With the garden and the pool I was in heaven, a totally contented human being. Sam adored the place, Blenheim adored it, Leslie came down from Boston with her golden retriever, Jack. They adored it. Steve, his wife, and my grandson Jamie came for a week in the summer, and they adored it. What more could I ask? What more could I want? The house, the big purchase, was worth it; it was a success. I might have liked to have sheep grazing—not too many; just a small family to complete the English-countryside picture. Would you say I was a visual person?

This was a place that attracted birds. I purchased every kind of bird feeder the Audubon Society had and proceeded to put them on all sides of the house. The birds came, I'll say that for them. I sent away for a purple-martin house—a double-decker hotel. It was put up high toward the top of the garden where I could see it clearly. I had visions of a purple martin in every one of its rooms, but I must confess to total failure. From that day to this more than ten years have passed, and nary a purple martin has registered in that hotel.

I put an Audubon book in every room and one near my chair at the breakfast table so I could look out the window and identify whatever flew by. The bird feeders had been placed in full view of the window, hanging on a post I'd had specially built. I bought every book on herbs, every book on flowers and trees. In my life, attention must be paid to detail. With precision, I had every aspect of my vision of "country" life represented. Not only was attention paid; manic attention was paid.

I realized after my first summer with the pool that there was no place to change clothes. For about a year I stubbornly stuck to my original plan of no pool house, knowing all the while I would have to capitulate. Anyway, the stage was set; there was already an equipment shed. A fine local carpenter designed the other half just like it, with room for a shower, sink, and loo, and a connecting section to house outdoor furniture, mats, etc. It was ideal and, once built, looked as though it had been there forever. Then followed the wisteria vine climbing up one side, climbing roses up the center wall, with dwarf evergreens and a weeping elm in front; beautiful. Then, of course, the pool house needed antique blue-and-white tiles for the sink top and some wicker and old wood furniture for the covered porch. To top it off, what else but a weather vane? One simply must have a weather vane. I chose a flying goose—how's that for fulfilling the need for a sense of permanence, solidity, not to mention the final visual touch?

While all this was being done, I decided it was also the moment to fix my bedroom. I had planned on that from the beginning, but as you may guess, none of this work was assigned to others. Garvin and I made the rounds of fabric and wallpaper houses, and since the bath was to be redone too, it was worked on at the same time. Garvin had a source for old beams, I chose a beautiful, wildly expensive wallpaper, and we were off and running. Everything I did to that house made it better. For a long time I went every weekend. Sometimes when I was able I'd take a week off and work on my book; then I spent a month in the summer correcting galleys. Buying that house had been the right thing to do, I was sure of it.

Sunset was a beautiful time. And the quiet of the morning. And the air. We mustn't forget the air, clear and clean; and, a two-minute drive away, the beach, where Blenheim and I would walk. The only drawback, as I finally became aware, was that I had to deal with everything myself.

I stayed with those improvements and made no more, except for buying two more acres. So I now had a total of three. For privacy and protection. Of course, it all had to be fenced in for Blenheim. And next I had to have a gazebo. Tony Walton, who has designed some of the theater's and film's most memorable sets, has an eye that can't be beat. He had seen and brought me a picture of one that was near Sag Harbor—a beauty, very English, rustic, octagonal in shape—and the carpenter to go with it. I had visions of myself sitting out there communing with nature, far from the madding crowd, and writing. A gloriously appealing vision. Wonderful what an imagination can do.

I installed a hammock between two trees overlooking the pool. Made a little walkway, with a bench, more azaleas, and hostas on one side, and another, with a variety of hostas, grasses, bamboo, and a Himalayan pine tree, on the other. That area led to the orchard, with apple trees and a vegetable and herb garden. A perfect picture of ideal country living, couple living, family living.

But I was *not* a couple; I had Sam and Blenheim, the regulars, and Steve and Leslie, the occasional visitors. Then Leslie moved to California and hasn't seen the house since, and Steve was working in Connecticut and had his own family, so it really was a house inhabited by me and Blenheim, who shared equal time there, and Sam, who came home from school on every holiday and the occasional weekend.

It had been on my mind for some time, from the beginning, really, that I would have to enlarge the kitchen. Since I am not a great cook, you might well ask why. My only answer would be that it is part of my fantasy—and I love sitting in kitchens. Go figure. Also, oddly enough, when Sam was around with his friends, there was no place for me to work. I should have sensed danger.

In my profession, whenever you plan anything that involves large sums of money, either a film or a play pays for it—that is, the proceeds thereof. Would you call that living on the edge—or adding on the edge? My autobiography bought two acres of land. As for my next project, I had it all figured out. I was about to embark on my second musical for Broadway, *Woman of the Year*. There are no guarantees, but my instinct told me it would be a success. And if it worked, I could add on to the house. At least I could think about it.

The addition was to be a large room—cathedral ceiling, old wooden beams, skylights again, fireplace, with sliding glass doors

opening onto a small brick patio for quiet contemplation when summer breezes blow. There was also to be an adjoining bath, which
would have in it everything I've always wanted to have: a steam
shower, a Jacuzzi for two, a bidet, great closets, a place for a small
electric stove and sink unit, for tea-making purposes on cold winter
afternoons. Ideally this should be a master bedroom, but as there is
not a lot that is ideal in this world, it would remain my workroom.
Again, landscaping would be involved and money would flow through
my fingers nonstop. And I would get to buy more furniture on my
travels, which would make me feel permanent. As I review all this, I
cannot believe how cavalier my attitude was about this addition. Having been raised believing—and still believing—that a life without
work is an empty life, how is it that I have continually had my earnings
spent almost before I earned them? I have always felt that somehow I
could, would, be able to make a living. As I've grown older and
witnessed the disappearance of friends and acquaintances of all ages
from my world, I realize that this is not necessarily true. But I am
determined and I'm willing to try almost anything. I'm persistent, I'm
talented, I'm a contributor to this planet, not merely a visitor—but
the reality is, I am not totally the master of my own fate. I could be
perfection itself in all conceivable areas, but if there are no roles (and
there aren't many), and if the powers that be (they are unnameable,
because they change with alarming frequency) don't want me, I will
indeed *not* be able to make that living. And that would be not only
unpleasant for me but disastrous. However, once a cavalier thinker,
always a cavalier thinker.

It started. But the bulldozers couldn't bulldoze until the
ground had thawed, and the work would have to be finished before
it froze again. That involved heavy coordinating of the mason for
breezeways, walkways, etc., the carpenters, electrician, plumber,
landscaper. See what one seemingly fairly simple "go ahead" can do?
It's called "in over your head"—mine, to be precise.

Like Topsy, the house grew and grew. Ideas spilled over,
one idea led to another. To add to my romantic country fantasy, there

The front view of the house that I built, loved, lived in for more than fifteen years, and am now ready to pass on to another family.

were large windows on either side of my giant Jacuzzi, so I could see all the flora and fauna that rested outside; wouldn't it be marvelous to have a birdbath outside? I could watch them bathe and they could watch me. What a picture!

I was advised that the water would stagnate and the birds would not be attracted to it. So what started as a birdbath became a small rock pool with a waterfall above. Enchanting. The motor kept the water moving and clean, and the birds loved it. There was one catch, as it turned out. On my first venture into the glorious bath, having laid out my best Porthault bath sheets and set the timer for the water jet, into the tub I stepped. The stage was set—trees, shrubs, waterfall in place and running, birds flying back and forth, bathing, drinking, flapping their wings. It was perfect. Then I pushed the button to start the water jet, and all hell broke loose. The birds heard the whooshing water through the window and flew away. Of course, that meant I couldn't have my whirling bath and my birds too, which meant the only way we could share the bathing moment was in silence, broken only by the sound of their waterfall. Another pipe dream shot to hell.

The view from my writing table was quite spectacular, rather European. Through the glass door was an allée of lawn as far as the eye could see. It led to the orchard, and en route on either side were rhododendrons, laurel, azaleas, lily of the valley, your occasional jack-in-the-pulpit, ferns, forsythia, epimedium, blood Japanese maples, a bench with a weeping mulberry shading its one corner. The best thing about the garden was that it was surprising. At almost every turn you'd come upon something unexpected, either a resting place or another trail or a tree. It really is special, though not fancy, because all of it looks natural. And I was proud of it—so proud that I decided everyone should see it, everyone being my friends, people I cared for whose homes I'd been to endlessly and who had never been to mine. Not like a payback; I just thought it was time, so I planned an outdoor summer Sunday lunch. Steve and his family came for that weekend, and Sam too, so there was some family representation. There must

have been seventy-five people there, and it was a perfect day. I really
loved having my house and lawn covered with people, and I wondered
why I didn't do it more often. All adored the garden and my new
wing. Many jokes about the bathtub for two. The house was complete.
Even the front gate, which had always been impossible, had been
redone, and it worked. I felt it was time, effort, and money well
invested—until I toted up the final bill, which came to more than the
cost of the original house. However, it was done, and it was beautiful
and enormously pleasure-giving. So I was set now. The house had
everything I wanted except for a garage, and I wasn't sure about that.
I'd managed for six years without one, so why bother? I spent a great
deal of time in my kitchen, not cooking so much as rearranging pots
and pans, baskets, jars, adding and taking away.

When I was on tour with *Woman of the Year* in the fall of
1983, Garvin called me one day with bad news. Somehow a squirrel
or a raccoon had got caught in the chimney of my new room. Heat
and dust had backed up into the room, and every drawer and closet
was pitch black, covered with soot. The room was wrecked. He had
found an incredible man who ran a service for calamities such as this,
and if anyone could restore the room, he could. I could not believe it;
the room was little more than a year old. Garvin's description was
hair-raising. By the time I returned to New York and arranged to meet
with the man who'd dealt with the damage, it was close to finished—
the restoration, that is. Close to, not entirely. My brand-new beautiful
pine floor had to be completely redone, scraped and varnished; every
piece of upholstered furniture had to be cleaned more than once;
inside every drawer, black soot would come off on your fingers, even
months after it was supposedly all gone. Cushions destroyed, lamp-
shades, my beautiful tub and shower—that soot had seeped into every
aperture, no matter how small. To call it depressing is a major under-
statement. And of course it took a while before I felt able to spend
time in that space. Finally the dead raccoon was behind me, and I
started to use all of my house again. But I never did get into the
entertaining habit. And as Sam's own life took shape, as he got older,

he came out less often. When he was there, I loved it all again, but that was because there was not only someone in the house with me but someone I could do everything for. That's what makes a house live and, finally, what makes it a home—people again. Can't do without them.

Gradually the negatives began to emerge. Plants would die and have to be replaced. Storms would raise havoc with trees, some of which would die or fall over or both. Bill would have to be called. The roof was leaking, call a roof man; the sink was leaking, call the plumber; outside lights didn't work properly or didn't give enough light, call the electrician; the pool filter was on the blink; the pond motor wasn't performing properly; the patrol people weren't patrolling. Finally it seemed to me that all I did was spend my weekends on the phone, contacting whomever I could reach to fix all of the above. Then the voles and/or moles took over. Mice had eaten the roots of my beautiful cherry tree, my apple trees, call the tree men. The bills began arriving with alarming frequency and added up to a tremendous expense.

I remember one Sunday morning, rising early, dressing hurriedly so I could get to Brent's around the corner to buy the Sunday *Times*. Rushing back, turning on the coffee, rushing to the TV for "Meet the Press." After that program and "This Week with David Brinkley," I clearly remember taking the newspapers and stretching out on the chaise, with Blenheim at my feet. Sun streaming through the window. After a while I looked up; the house was empty, and I thought, What am I doing here? I looked at Blenheim and said, "This is ridiculous. Why are we here? Why do we rush to the country every weekend, when nobody cares if we're here or not?"

I began to review my pattern on arrival. It went something like this: Enter house—turn off alarm quickly before it goes off— put food in fridge—unpack clean laundry brought from the city: the schlepping never ends. Turn on hot water—gas—light the lights— open the windows—let the house live: as though it is constantly inhabited. Fill birdfeeders—hurry back into house so you can sit and watch them as they arrive. Create an atmosphere. This was a ridiculous exercise. I went there to relax, and relax was the last thing I did. By the time I had finished all of the above, I was exhausted. And the day was half gone.

That was the beginning of my facing the fact: perhaps it might be time to move on. The romance was all but over.

Then too, as I had to travel endlessly for work, I spent less and less time there. I also spent less and less time in New York. And I *enjoyed* weekends in New York. They gave me an opportunity to wander the streets leisurely, go to the Village, do all the things I could never do when I was in a play. But I felt guilty staying in New York when the house was sitting empty in Amagansett.

In 1985 I agreed to go to London to appear in Tennessee Williams's *Sweet Bird of Youth*, to be directed by Harold Pinter. That would entail my being out of the United States for nine months, during which time I would see neither New York nor Amagansett. And the children, being scattered as they were, wouldn't inhabit the country house often either. Both establishments had to be maintained, of course, as though I were there.

After my nine months in England, I had two weeks at home for Christmas with my family. Then to Australia for four and a half months in *Sweet Bird*. That meant fourteen months without setting foot in Amagansett. Then coming back for my son Sam's wedding. Life has a way of taking over. I spent some time in the country and then had to start planning and rehearsing for the American production of *Sweet Bird*. So in a four-year period, from the *Woman of the Year* tour on, I had been home for roughly eight months of divided time in city and country. I had to work to pay for everything. I had to travel to work. Simple arithmetic, and the garden was growing, and the fact that it was a burden was becoming more and more apparent.

As a result, the laughs were fewer, the smiles less smilier, more and more the obstacles reared their ugly heads, and pretty soon everything became an obstacle. My patience factor, which never was great, became even less so. Suddenly there were days when everything was a chore, when going out there was a chore. Going to the country became like climbing that mountain: because it's there.

I love the country. I need nature, things growing; I especially need the sea. But if I have to deal with every nut and bolt, diseased tree and plant, leaky pipe, the joy slowly disappears. There is a time element in there as well. If all my time is spent dealing with the kitchen of life, then when do I read, walk, listen to music, or just plain enjoy and not have to worry about cost? The answer is, a woman alone has no business owning two establishments. Not unless she's rich. A family does, couples do. You see, it all comes back to that.

I have spent years living as though I were a couple. I was born, as we all were, into a society where couples rule. To be half of a pair is what it's all about. Well, I had decided years ago, after several failed relationships, that I'd rather be alone any day than be attached to someone I wasn't attached to; at least I'd have freedom and my self-respect. Being alone is great in so many ways. I can choose when I want to eat and what, I can read my morning paper in peace without having to make conversation (I hate *making* conversation anytime, but especially in the morning). I can sleep when I choose and wake when I choose, I can walk around the house with my hair in rollers and cream on my face if I choose. Naturally, there are drawbacks. It is lonely. And one doesn't want to spend one's life pleasing only oneself. Of course, in my work there is much one does that is part of the job, and a great deal of time can be spent bowing to the wishes of others. So it's often a relief to be on one's own.

The couple syndrome became glaringly apparent to me in the country. I have been aware of it for years in small doses, but I guess the isolation of country living and the greater dependency on others brought it home to me in a whole new way. Mind you, it's the most natural thing in the world for one couple to say to another, "Let's the four of us go to a movie or have dinner next week or come on over for Scrabble" (if anyone still plays Scrabble). It's natural and understandable. There are few men content to spend an evening with their wives and another woman, and there are few wives content to

spend an evening with their husbands and another woman. Occasionally, perhaps, but only that. So although I have great friends who
enjoy my company and God knows I do theirs, they don't often think
in terms of just me to make a threesome. Not your average way to
spend an evening, three not being anyone's favorite number. The odd
numbers are called that because that's what they are: odd.

I don't blame them, I don't blame anyone. That's just the
way it is. And as I've never been one who found it easy to call and say,
"I'm here," I spent more time than I wished alone in the country.
And I also became somewhat paranoid. Small dinners I wasn't invited
to where my friends would all be, but not me. Large parties I wasn't
invited to where everyone would be, but not me. Nobody planned it.
But it did make me feel more lonely, more unwanted, and less eager
to be in the country. It also brought home to me that I must make
new friends who were solo to add to the old. I was not going to live
that planned weekend life, not ever.

In addition, it spooked me to be in the country alone at
night. The days were great, no problem; but when the sun went down,
the scenario changed. That goes back to my childhood. Hearing foot-
steps down the hall while in bed at night and covering my head so I
wouldn't hear. Seeing shadows of passing cars on the wall and
imagining people hidden in my apartment while alone in my bed
in the Village. A creaking floor signifying a footstep; a tree hitting the
roof, making my heart skip a beat. Crazy, I know, but somewhere
many moons ago I was frightened by something at night, and it never
left me.

In 1987 I was going to be filming in Israel from May until
June or July, after which I would rush to Newport, Rhode Island, for
another film, which would take up the summer. It was time to face
more facts. Rent for July and August, then the house would pay for
itself the rest of the year. What a good idea! I was nervous about it,
not wanting to see majolica crashing all around me, or burns in chairs
and sofas, but the time had come. I had to do it.

The month of April was spent putting away the valuables,

locking my clothes in closets. Sorting out and putting away is never much fun, but I pressed on, and instead of thinking of my house and how someone might violate it, I concentrated on my trip to Israel and my first movie in seven years. And so there was no garden planting or planning that year. No point with me away. Just do the bare minimum. My withdrawal continued.

Abroad, in Israel, I was much too interested, excited, and curious about where I was and what I was seeing to even think about my house, much less miss it. Without a push or a shove from me, or at least without a conscious one, the weaning had begun.

And when I returned to New York I found I wanted to stay there, I didn't want to rush out to the country. But I had to go. Remember, it was there. And I had to see what damage had been done by departing tenants. Perhaps I didn't want to see damage to the house I built. Perhaps I already felt it was no longer completely mine, now that strangers had lived in it. Unfortunately, my first rental was not a rousing success. One floor (the pine one again, can you believe it?) had to be redone, outdoor furniture was broken, upholstery stained, more damage in two months than had been done in ten years. People are careless.

Yet despite my disappointment in the tenants, I found I loved being there out of season. Amagansett became more of a village, less a resort, more my style. I was happy to have my self-made nest back, though I didn't take out most of the things I'd put away. The house didn't need them. One of my great mistakes was that I had had too much expensive furniture out there. Antiques, good ones; a majolica collection, Audubons—too much for a house that finally I wasn't in often enough and that would have strangers in it from July to Labor Day. So except for a few little touches, I left it as it was. I thought, I'll only be renting it again next year and have to go through the same damn routine all over again.

Next I had to go to L.A. on business—again, packing, airports, hotels. I finally figured out that another reason for my reluctance to go to the country was that I spent so much time moving from one place to another in my work that when I finally did get home, I wanted to stay put and not pack up again.

No sooner did I finish my work in L.A. than I was heading for four months of filming in England. Sam and Suzy were able to use the house occasionally, but only that, as either one or the other of them was often away working.

I was able to rent it for the summer, this time with a known reliable tenant. And there were some days in August when I could have gone there, but of course it was occupied.

After a sane meeting with my business manager, it became clear that I was in my house so infrequently that it made little or no sense for me to keep it. For years Steve had been telling me to sell it, Garvin had told me to sell it, and I had bucked them both. Now the moment of truth was upon me—badly timed, as usual. The negatives were all too clear, but there were positives. There were parts of me in that house. And I did love it when I was there. But I had fulfilled my need for putting a house together and making it breathe, and for creating a garden that was a place for local birds to gather, feed, drink, and bathe, and was a place of beauty as well. Yes, perhaps it was time to move on. It's a funny thing about my house: once I had faced the fact that *my* life was not really *that* life, once I had decided to eliminate my house, even though it is still beautiful, still my creation, it became *the* house. Emotionally I had left it, and taken with me the happy memories of time well spent and wonderful things done. It is the one and only time that I completely made a house my own, so it had a special meaning for me. But the wrenching was past—it went with the decision made. So go ahead, Bacall, take a deep breath, close your eyes to Sam's wanting me to hang on a bit longer, forget sentiment. *Sell!*

And that's what I've done. Sam thinks I'll regret it, my friend Mary Stone thinks I'll regret it. Perhaps I will. But I can always have something else, at another time in another place, or I can have that month in Tuscany, travel up the Nile, or sit in a flat in London or Paris. Give myself endless surprises, indulge in last-minute whims.

I don't want to spend the rest of my life worrying about house maintenance. Body maintenance will occupy me enough, I am sure.

So I've taken the big plunge. Having sold (it's only taken
close to three years), I'll be open to everything, anything. If I've made
the wrong choice, there will be other houses—and if I haven't, I'll be
free.

# ACTING

Musing about my career in the theater, I wondered if I would ever have a high onstage again, one even close to the high of *Applause*. I knew there could never be a repeat of that feeling, because that was my first musical; the first anything is always unforgettable. I would never forget how I felt in *Applause*. I reveled in the response that came to me from those audiences. I yearned to have that feeling again. Who wouldn't want to recapture that rush of warmth and affection wafting over the orchestra pit and footlights and hitting you right between the eyes from your first appearance onstage through the final curtain call? Yes, it was approval, that sense of being wanted, of having finally accomplished at least some of what you set out to accomplish when you made that first childish, romantic decision to become an actress. Indeed, why *wouldn't* you want to feel again that you were using every inch of yourself, every cell was working, every sense was alive and thriving? Yet the older I get, the more elusive all this seems to become, as the older I get, the more demanding it becomes, the more difficult to find wonderful projects.

I've had such an odd career—many more downs than ups, yet some dazzling ups. It seems, on sober reflection (a mistake to indulge in at the best of times), to have been an uphill claw most of the last forty-odd years—it's forty-six years, actually—and that's a horrifying fact. It means that even after forty-six years I haven't reached that pinnacle. I'm still out there trying to please, trying to attain what I haven't attained, hoping to be noticed, hoping for a good job. Even trying to decide where and how I want to live. Will dissatisfaction— restlessness—insecurity never cease?

Yet I'm called a legend by some, a title and category I am less than fond of. Aren't legends dead? Isn't that what makes a legend, not being around anymore? Or sometimes I'm called a special lady of films and theater, which makes me feel like a dowager empress. If I knew how a dowager empress felt. So if I am these things, why do I worry so much? I feel such angst because in my slightly paranoiac head, legends and special ladies don't work; it's over for them; they just go around being legends and special ladies. But I, poor fool, still care, still hope, still enjoy, and I must also, somewhere in the deep recesses of my brain, still believe that my time will come around again.

At the beginning of the end of work I am always happy to be home. The main problem with stopping work, particularly stopping musical work, is that when the eight shows a week stop, so do the body warm-ups. I always tell myself that I'll go back to them, I won't let my body fall apart. But my body often has its own ideas. And I am so bone tired at the end of a run, I just want to flop. I remember having a conversation with Henry Fonda about that once, and his telling me that at the end of his run in *Mister Roberts*, he went to Jamaica, fell on a beach, and slept for two weeks. We don't realize how much energy we put out every day. The only opportunity we have to refuel is when we finish a run; that one day off a week we get doesn't allow us to let go completely. After the discipline of a show, it's great, a luxury, to have no schedule. People who live regular lives cannot understand one's unwillingness to commit to social engagements weeks in advance. I flatly refuse. I decided a long time ago that I had to have freedom of choice, had to see what mood I was in. If indeed I wanted to go to dinner at all.

When I think about acting, I think first of drama school—my first one was the New York School of the Theatre, on Saturdays only, when I was in high school, then the American Academy of Dramatic Arts, full-time, after I graduated—where a certain kind of learning begins: technique. You're supposed to learn this so it becomes a part of you, without having to think. For me, dramatic school was the start of a loss of self-consciousness, only the start. Many different classes—first—the *voice*: breathing (from the diaphragm; no heaving chest), enunciation, and projection, register (high–low), then the *body*—grace—moving from door to table to chair without bumping into anything. Posture—up and down stairs with a book on your head (just as you've seen it in the movies)—it may sound tedious, and it often is, but it's also basic and necessary. Remember these instruments are essential tools of an actor. To have a voice with range—not abrasive—that an audience can listen to for two or three hours straight. And to move so your body belongs to you—effortlessly. The main function of an actor is to interpret, to project the author's intention to the audience; the playwright, after all, speaks through the actor. I used to think that if *I* felt it, that would be enough—not so. It doesn't matter how much *I* feel it; the *audience* must feel it. That doesn't mean you feel nothing; of course you do. You can't help it—if you think, really think, and if you tell the truth. I never found a formula that would enable me to get to the root of the character. Each one is different. Each one requires an individual approach.

In my first speaking part on the stage, I was lucky to have George Kaufman as my director. He was very simpatico, admired actors, was articulate in his direction, and gave it quietly. I never saw him embarrass anyone in the company. Over the years, I have seen some directors attack actors, humiliate them in front of their fellow workers—a loathsome trait, most often confined to directors of small talent. Mike Curtiz, who was a master with the camera, in his frustration—his inability to articulate what he wanted—he sometimes lost patience with an actor, but in his case, I guess in all cases, actors got in his way. I've never worked with a really good director who was anything but kind and instilled trust in me—a prerequisite for any performance at all. Anyway, in that first play, *Franklin Street*, I was too nervous to analyze much of anything. I just did whatever Kaufman told me, though during the rehearsal period, as he welcomed an exchange of ideas, I must have made some contribution to the interpretation of my role. The play was a comedy, my character was in a constant dream state, poetically oriented, and spoke accordingly, so she was funny as well. Comedy has been instinctive for me, always. I don't mean joke-telling comedy, I mean comedy arising from situations and based on true emotions.

When I got to Hollywood, I was a year older than in *Franklin Street* but still not wildly experienced. After meeting and talking with me, Howard Hawks decided my screen test would be a scene from Rose Franken's play *Claudia*. I had auditioned for and been offered the part of understudy on the national tour, so I knew the play and had some familiarity with Claudia herself. Claudia was a young, happily married woman who discovers almost simultaneously that she is pregnant and that her beloved mother is dying of cancer. It is a play about growing up, dealing with loss. I had experienced no personal losses at that time. I was the tender age of eighteen. I remember feeling frightened. First, I was frightened of Howard Hawks; second, I was frightened of the camera and all the people behind it and around it. I felt they knew everything, while I knew nothing. It did, however, help that I knew the play, had already studied the part. Acting in front of a camera had nothing to do with what I learned at drama school. I had studied for the stage.

In movies, you have to deliver the emotion immediately and often—for the long shot, for the medium shot, for the close-up. I recall my pounding heart and shaking hands, but I also recall how much I enjoyed, as the day wore on, playing the scenes with Charlie Drake, even with the monster eye of the camera on us and the two eyes of Hawks on me. It was an intimate scene, so it was almost as if we were the only ones there, almost as if there were no crew, no cameraman; just us, almost. It made a difference. Hawks, of course, had a tremendous amount to do with my feeling; he took such care with every shot, and this test was for a contract with him, so my future was riding on it. Little did I know to what extent. That was my first experience with movie acting, and it took me years to feel comfortable again in front of a camera. Actually, I think I'm just now beginning to have a clue. The quiet and the intimacy of the scene I was playing made it possible for me to give more, to almost become that girl, though it was only a day's shooting and with the preparation it all added up to maybe a week. But for that time I felt like Claudia. With each passing hour during that week—through osmosis, plus working with Hawks—some of Claudia seeped into my pores. And though our backgrounds differed, I was still able to identify with her enough, not to be marvelous in the part, but enough to do it well. And enough to be signed to a personal contract with Howard Hawks. The trembling emotion that went through my entire body was there as I placed my mother where Claudia's mother was. The thought of losing my mother was so painful that the pain filtered through in the scene. I was taught in drama school to draw upon life, to bring as close a comparison as possible and use it all. At eighteen, there's not a lot of life to draw upon, but there are always ways to find some parallel to that person you are playing. Well, maybe not always, but most of the time. And the director is there to help.

When I tested for *To Have and Have Not*, the story was different, completely different. Slim was a young woman who'd knocked around a lot in her life, a woman of the world, a woman with humor, with insolence, who in traveling alone had developed a certain veneer as protection against the men who preyed on her. I had not one thing in common with her except humor. Of course, all through this period Hawks had been regaling me with stories of actresses he'd directed, how he had them behave in love scenes, reacting as a man would, independent, with double entendre being stressed continually. I didn't have a clue how to behave like a man, and being a woman of the world conjured up images of dark alleys, sex (I knew little about that), and seedy characters. Hawks gave me a script to memorize. I couldn't imagine, really imagine, how I would play this part; it was an exercise in playacting in the beginning, sort of like dressing up. How could I play a woman when I was a girl? How could I have the upper hand in an exchange with a man when I knew so little about them, was still a virgin? How could I be insolent and independent when I was terrified? When I went through it with Howard, I obviously pretended that I knew a hell of a lot more than I did. I made up my mind then that I would just do it; I had to do it if I wanted the part, and I wanted the part. I listened very carefully to Howard, went home, and practiced alone in front of a mirror—not to see how I looked so much as to try to feel there was someone else there.

In the test, everything I wore was carefully chosen by Howard, and the makeup man and the hairdresser were told what to do by Howard. John Ridgely, a terrific supporting actor at Warner Bros., was in the scene with me; he, too, was told what to do by Howard. That was the start of Howard's making me into his concept of the ideal woman. My terrible shyness would not go away, and curiously, that helped in the scene; my own vulnerability was apparent. I hadn't planned it; it was just so much a part of me that I couldn't leave it behind. I acted the way Howard wanted me to. That was the first awakening I had: how to become somebody else—somebody who had a past, a present, and a future, who went beyond the single-scene characters I had played in drama school. My sense of humor saved me, as it always has, and it had a great deal to do with the character, Slim.

When I finally did get that part and the movie was under way, that's when I began to be more aware of some of the essentials. However, I occasionally found myself falling into a pattern where instead of listening to the actor I was in the scene with, I would say the lines I had learned and then just wait for the other actor to say his.

I didn't even know I was doing it. When Bogie was in the scene and saw that I was just standing there, rather blank, he'd change his line or he'd say "What?" That shook me up. I'd say, "Why did you do that?" He'd say, "Because you weren't listening." I soon found out the difference between listening and hearing what's being said and just standing there and saying my lines. Seems ridiculously simple. But my nerves had taken over. I was so afraid of missing my cue that I wasn't thinking at all—wasn't listening at all—just waiting for the word that would lead me to my next line. When I really listened, I didn't have to think of my hands or my feet, what they were doing; I was responding to the words being spoken, so hands and feet took care of themselves. Hands can't just hang there at the end of your arms—they must have life, and that does not mean constant movement. What a simple thing! And what a marvelous way to learn it! Bogie was so sharp as an actor, he missed nothing. He was always aware of what everyone was doing. I found that when he made me snap to, I was immediately changed. My posture changed—all antennae up. I was in control of what I was doing, and it wasn't an accident.

Once, during the filming of *To Have and Have Not*, I had worked the entire day with Hoagy Carmichael and many extras, shooting my song "How Little We Know." It was a day of steady and enjoyable work, and at the end of it Howard commended me on how well I'd done. But I had no idea what I'd done that was so different from the other days except concentrate and do what I was told to do. I never did understand the compliment, unless it was based on my having no distractions (the main one being Bogart) and totally focusing on the subject at hand and Howard himself.

When Hawks said, "Action," I would start the scene as rehearsed. One day on *The Big Sleep*, the scene was this: doorbell rings in the Sternwood house, the butler goes to the door, and I (Vivian Sternwood) come out of my room and head for the door, behind which Bogie, as Philip Marlowe, is standing. On cue, I moved, could be seen emerging from the hidden room, walking toward the front door. Something went wrong, and we had to do it again. Whereupon Bogie came up to me and said, "Where are you coming from?" "My bedroom," I said. "Weren't you doing something before the doorbell rang? You don't just walk to the door because the director says 'Action.' " I have never forgotten that. Another lesson: preparation. That's what acting is, really—no breast-beating, no big motivation discussions, just thought, focus, logical thinking of where you are, where you were before, and why you are there. And listening. And truth. Most of all, acting is about telling the truth.

How long an actress lives professionally depends on her stamina, the extent of her masochism, her imagination, and her yearning for recognition or approval. I don't know which of these has been most heavily featured in my career, but I do know I have called upon all of these gifts and have thrown in a few more.

Sometime around 1952 or '53, I had approached Darryl Zanuck, head of 20th Century–Fox, about a play called *The Greeks Had a Word for It*, by Zoë Akins. George Cukor had told me it would make an excellent movie, with a terrific part for me. Zanuck, to his credit, bought it, and it became *How to Marry a Millionaire*, adapted and produced by Nunnally Johnson and directed by Jean Negulesco. For unfathomable reasons, Cukor was eliminated as a possible director. Typical Hollywood (and possible unavailability). Nunnally, who was my great, great friend, told me he wanted me for one of the starring parts, but as I'd never been filmed playing comedy, I would have to test for it. Didn't he know I was the one who brought the property to Zanuck? He was sensitive to me and my feelings, knew it was not the norm to ask an established star to test for a part, said there was no doubt in his mind that I would get the part, but the powers that be wanted to see me on film. My heart sank. My career was not going brilliantly at the time. I had just bought my way out of my Warner Bros. contract. This would be a great break for me. But suppose I didn't get it after making the test? Suppose I failed? Yet I had no choice, I had to take that chance, so I said yes. I thought of other stars, and I use the word advisedly, whom they wouldn't have dared ask test, but my entire career had been like that—one long never-ending test. Still is. So with a small amount of resentment, a huge amount of false bravado, and an oversize measuring cup of anxiety, I tested for the part of Schatze, the leader of the group of three women on the search. Jean Negulesco, another friend, and the director of the test, was all sympathy. I was nervous, but I got through it. It is a weird feeling—that determination to do it well, to be a pro, to bring something new to it, to surprise "them," combined with keeping resentment and defensiveness and a sense of inadequacy out of sight, out of the way, and hoping no one will see how desperately you want the part. I have always been envious and somewhat in awe of actors who always seem able to get the parts they want. I'd give a lot to know how to do it, but the truth is, I don't know how, and any attempt to push myself would only end in disaster and unemployment.

At the end of the day I left the set, drove off the Fox lot, smiled at all and sundry, appeared confident and at ease, not knowing how many days I would have to wait before "they" saw it and decided and then somebody told me. Nerve-racking, tense-making, life-shortening. I spent what seemed an inordinate amount of time waiting for the word. "They" do take their time. A weekend got in the way of an immediate decision. I tried valiantly not to think about it every waking minute, not to jump every time the telephone rang. I told myself endless stories: one, I hadn't heard because the test was lousy and Nunnally didn't have the heart to call me; two, I hadn't heard because while the test was okay, someone had just thought of somebody else who would be "great," if they could get her; or finally, and closer to reality, I hadn't heard because they hadn't seen it yet. My priority was most assuredly not theirs. Torture! I wished I hadn't wanted it so much. My entire future seemed to hinge on my getting this part. Could one part be so important? Of course not, but when you want something badly, and when your work life is not moving right along, and when there is a singular lack of urgency for your services on the part of a studio, you begin to believe that *everything* depends on one part. By the time the call came from Nunnally, telling me, "Hooray, you've got the part. Darryl loved the test, as did we all. Congratulations!" I had built such a case against myself I was surprised I didn't say, You can keep your part, I don't want it.

*The Robe* was advertised as being the first picture shot in

CinemaScope because it was a Zanuck production. And *How to Marry a Millionaire* was released after it so as not to conflict. Anyway, it was a ghastly new out-of-proportion process designed to attract moviegoers. The dimensions were unflattering, but I loved CinemaScope for one reason—a scene was played all the way through, be it two pages or four. There was very little cutting to medium shots, closeups, and over the shoulder, so a scene had a beginning, a middle, and an end. Heaven for me.

Even after *How to Marry a Millionaire* there were still questions about my being able to play comedy. When *Designing Woman* was going to be made, I called Dore Schary, who was producing it, to tell him I knew I could do it. (The part had been written for Grace Kelly, but she married a prince instead.) I swallowed pride and anything else that got in the way to get that part. For some reason, a test was not mentioned, but Gregory Peck, the leading man, had the right to approve his leading lady, which he did, thank heaven. So I got it. But it hadn't been easy.

Some years later, my friend Leland Hayward called to offer me the lead in a play, *Goodbye Charlie*, written by my friend George Axelrod. Leland was a persuasive man. "You'll have every protection, eight weeks out of town, you'll start voice lessons, so projection will be automatic and there'll be no chance of your losing your voice through strain, nerves, or bad breathing. Read it; you'll love it." I was deep in the heart of Spain, filming, and, after nine months of living in London, had to decide whether to stay and keep my two children, Stephen and Leslie, in school there or to return to the United States. Either way represented a new beginning for me, the making of a life without Bogie. It was 1959. And I really liked the play, which was about two men, Charlie and George, rogues with women, who prefer the company of other men. They were macho guys to whom women meant sex—objects not to be taken too seriously. Charlie is caught in the act with some-one's wife on a yacht, is shot while escaping through the porthole, and is washed up, on a beach. As punishment, he is brought back to earth as a woman. A far-out, crazy idea, but creative and funny—I thought.

As work seemed to be the decisive factor in my life at that point, at least geographically, there was nothing to do but accept. And I somehow felt it was fate—that offer told me where my future lay. New York, here I come—as Charlie, a macho ladies' man who one day finds himself reincarnated as me. And a very tricky situation it turned out to be. Of course, I was terrified. It is one thing to dream of being on the stage at the age of fifteen (when you're sure you can do anything), starting slowly, learning your craft. It is quite another to arrive on Broadway some eighteen years later, a known voice and face, and star in a play. Your first starring part. I wasn't thinking of critics or if the show would be a hit. I voiced my doubts to Leland, whom I rightfully trusted. Neither he nor George had any doubts, and the picture they painted was so positive, of such impending glory, it was impossible to resist. And with my everlasting romanticizing, fantasiz-ing about the theater, I thought that at last my first dream had come true. It was exciting. I was excited. The start of any project is the start of a new adventure for me. I don't seem to think much about details, I just hold my nose and jump. But I wasn't quite prepared for the amount of preliminary work involved. I love to work but had forgotten —had actually never known—how much had to be thought about before acting begins onstage. Voice, body work, breathing, projection, building and sustaining stamina. Emotions. Preparation.

The first reading of the play was traumatic. It was all in the hands of George and Leland, they were the theater pros. But the press had to be dealt with before we could focus on the play. Smile for the cameras, tell jokes. George Axelrod, writer-director; Leland Hayward, producer; Sydney Chaplin, costar. Nerve-racking. We were all happy with the project and with each other, never mind the stupid questions. How does it feel to be onstage? "I'll let you know when I get there."

How does it feel to be back in New York? "Perfectly natural." Would Bogie have approved of your doing this? "Doing what, staying alive? Oh, I do think so." I didn't realize then how often the Bogie question would be asked, and over how many years, no matter what I did; that in the eyes of the press I would always be attached to him.

With all that behind me, the next move was the play. We are all onstage. Center and downstage is a table, with a chair facing upstage for the director. Next to him, a chair for the stage manager and chair for the director's secretary and/or assistant. The director is facing a row of chairs where we, the actors, sit with script in hand. An Equity representative goes through the formality of reading the rules. Leland, our producer, greets us and sits in his chair to listen to the play. George, our director, tells us to relax, generally how he wants the play to be acted, explains the set to us, which is there in miniature —no, Oliver Smith, our set designer, explains his set. That is the fun part. George tells a funny theater joke; we laugh. He tells us to take it easy, he doesn't expect a performance. Easy for him to say. There is a huge silence before we begin. I am very nervous. We all are. I keep my head down, assume a physical attitude that seems to me to be professional. I notice that the pro stage actors take pencils for note taking, script marking. With great authority, I do the same. I hope my voice won't sound hollow, but when first I speak it doesn't sound like my voice as I have known it. I feel that I must deliver an almost performance. I feel that all eyes and ears are on me, waiting to see if I'm any good at all, and I think to myself, How the hell did I get into this? Help! Let me out! I feel shy, self-conscious, convinced I'm doing it all wrong. Boy, am I a case! Back to school. I have inflicted all this misery on myself, mind you. But with this play I am beginning to learn firsthand about theater and what it takes. What it's all about from an actor's point of view, what is expected of a star. And the responsibility of it! They are betting their futures on me. George, Leland, the other actors—oh, but I can't think about that, or I'll never be able to do it. So I don't. But as the reading progresses, the combination of all the above feelings plus the sound of the other actors playing their parts takes over. This will be the self-inflicted test. Can I do it? Can I be a stage actress? Life, mine in particular, has always been about taking chances. Bogie used to say, "I don't go to Las Vegas; I'm not that kind of gambler. I gamble with my life." And that is what I do. It's all well and good and safe to sit in a living room and say how good you are; it's quite another thing to get out there and find out. If I was going to fall on my face in this play, I was going to fall for all to see. And that *is* taking a chance.

When I was about to embark on my first live television appearance, in *The Petrified Forest*, David Selznick said to me, "Are you sure you're not making a mistake? If you are, you'll be making it in front of millions of people. Think about that." Very chancy. Right —yet I couldn't understand his thinking. Well, I could understand it; I just couldn't agree with it. How can you ever be that protected, that safe? I was protected only in the beginning—by Howard Hawks, then by Bogie, though never professionally by him after *The Big Sleep*. After that I'd been on my own. *The Petrified Forest* was to be an hour and a half long, and it was live. No chance to do it over. But if I didn't do it, how would I ever know if I could? Bogie was in it, re-creating his Duke Mantee role, and Henry Fonda was playing Alan Squier, a part originated by Leslie Howard. Impossible to refuse. So my risk taking was not bravery in my eyes. It was finding out about myself, what my limitations were, how much more there was to me than I had shown up to that time. In addition, that production was the start of my very valuable friendship with Henry Fonda.

That first foray into live television was terrifying. Not only did I have to know every word, but I had to hit every mark without anyone noticing and be aware of which of the four cameras was on. "Look for the red light." It was the worst of both worlds, stage and screen. We rehearsed for three weeks, but on D day, stomachache, headache, whatever, was out of the question. You *had* to do it. As we were live on the air, they started with a countdown. "Places." I was on at the very beginning, and I could hear ten . . . nine . . . eight . . . seven . . . six, etc., with my heart pounding so loud I was sure the microphone would pick it up. Waiting for them to pull the switches—hoping they would. Miraculously, I didn't forget my lines.

I found the red light. I got through it. I was Gaby, who dreamed of going to France but was stuck in a nowhere place on the road to the petrified forest, running a half-assed restaurant and gas station with her grandfather. All I had were my dreams and my books of poetry to give me hope. It was a part no one in the movie world would have cast me in—there were no jokes, no wisecracks, I was not in control. I was a romantic dreamer, and I was good, dammit. Robert Sherwood, playwright extraordinaire—it was his play, after all—was happy. Bill Paley of CBS was happy. Bogie was happy. Hank was happy. And I was happy. And thrilled I had lived through it.

My next big live television experience was playing Elvira in *Blithe Spirit*, with Noël Coward and Claudette Colbert. An enchanting play, written by Noël, it had been a great success onstage both here and in England. As a matter of fact, part of my usher's training—age sixteen—was at the Broadway production of *Blithe Spirit*, starring Clifton Webb. It was adapted for TV by Noël, and he was going to direct as well as play the central role. It was a comedy in the Coward mode, witty and original. Claudette played his second wife, and I the ghost of his first. I was dressed in gray chiffon by Don Loper, with a completely gray face and body, a gray wig, and bright-red lips and nails. We all were nervous, Noël doing three things at once, plus having an infection in his upper thigh which made it difficult for him to move. And as if it wasn't bad enough to be doing the entire play live, he insisted on inviting an audience of Hollywood elite: Hedda Hopper, Louella Parsons—the top and toughest columnists of the day—Elizabeth Taylor, Judy Garland, Bogie, of course, and on and on. A nightmare for me, total terror. The only wonderful thing about going through a hysterical time like that is the relief and exhilaration you feel when it's over. Live television was the best, with its immediacy—you had *one* chance, so with adrenaline pumping with a vengeance, everything working, you had to be good. But still, it was worth it.

With a play, there's the rehearsal period, the time of discovery, experimentation. During the *Goodbye Charlie* rehearsals, I felt better with each passing day. I was allowed to find my way, talking everything over with George. But his being my friend was inhibiting to me. I never felt really free to discuss the scenes. Some of them needed rewriting, and he was the writer. I was still taking voice lessons. Leland would walk all over the theater, the back of the orchestra, last row in the balcony, testing me, saying "I can't hear you"—his way of keeping me aware of projection, the importance of having every member of the audience hear the dialogue. It's funny that no matter how close a friendship, when work is involved, friendship changes. Leland is the producer, George is the director and author, I am the actress. The producer is management, so there is a tiny wall between us. In the theater, it's all exposed nerve ends anyway, and until you open, you are at your most vulnerable.

No one outside the theater knows what goes on during an out-of-town tryout. For me, the first disaster happened opening night in Pittsburgh. Theater dressing rooms being what they are, mostly inadequate, mine had a cement floor. At the end of the show, I started to sit at my dressing table, when my dresser, who was nervous and old, pulled the chair out instead of holding it to push in, whereupon down I went, my coccyx (tailbone) hitting the cement. It was painful and I couldn't move. Leland and George came rushing backstage to tell me how wonderful I was, found me immobile on the floor. So instead of festivities, doctors were summoned. I wore a brace for weeks after, and my coccyx has been floating ever since.

Forget glamour. I learned gradually that I'd have to pretty much forget my New York life, except for calls to my children and my mother, who was keeping a close eye. All I could do was rehearse in the day, then play at night, try not to confuse the new scenes George was writing with the ones I was playing for the paying customers. I was learning. I was building stamina. And I'd need it. I was tired, and I wasn't up to going out much after the show. In any event, I wasn't invited very often. The split between management and actors seemed to be built in. It was George and Leland together, with me not included. They'd be talking about the play, and actors' opinions were never needed, never wanted. After rehearsing new stuff during the day, Sydney Chaplin and I would sit in my dressing room before the show, going over and over our added lines. When you're sitting out front, it all looks so easy, such fun. Years ago, when my son Steve was in his teens, he used to say, "How can you be tired? You only work two and a half hours a day." It's hopeless to try to explain to *anyone*, much less your own child, the amount of time and energy invested before you walk on the stage, let alone the energy needed to spend two and a half hours onstage in front of an audience. In a comedy, the requirements are even greater. So much energy is required—in fact, you are on such a high—that it takes hours after a performance to unwind enough so you can get to sleep.

In the case of *Goodbye Charlie*, George Axelrod and Leland Hayward, who lived in New York and who'd spent lifetimes in the theater, were more concerned with critics, certainly more aware of them, than I was. Mind you, my idea of heaven is not to read reviews. If I could be like Katie Hepburn, who claims she's never read them, I'd be thrilled. But I feel compelled somehow. Even if the critics are as irrelevant as many are, I've been brought up in a world that says their opinions count, so I am as much a victim of their slings and arrows as anyone else. I've seen critics sleep, or should I say pass out, during an opening night. I've learned that quite a few critics are failed playwrights or novelists and are frustrated and bitter. One way to vent their anger is in a review: they can get back at producers, other writers, actors. They have the first word—they have the power; if we complain, it sounds like sour grapes. So it all boils down to a no-win situation. Except that a bad review hurts—it is painful, and it's killed many a career.

The obstacles never end. Thank heaven for Sydney Chaplin. I had him to commiserate with, and he was an old hand in the theater. I couldn't really discuss problems, unless they were acting problems, with George. Knowing my fears and anxieties, he'd been first-rate with me—solid, helpful. But he'd been under total, nonstop pressure. Between rewriting and directing, he'd not only had no sleep but was so close to the play and to us that he had to get away to see it clearly again. In addition to which, he had been the wunderkind of Broadway—he'd had nothing but hits since *The Seven Year Itch*. But

*Goodbye Charlie* was his first directorial effort. The rewriting went on as we moved from city to city. Rehearsing by day, playing at night, new hotel rooms, packing, unpacking, new theaters, new crews. I had never in my life had this experience, plus starring in a play headed for Broadway. Each theater was different. What was most important to my well-being was that the first row in the orchestra was not too close to the stage. I dreaded being able to see faces in the audience. I still dread it.

George left the ship for a few days and returned with an entirely new last scene, to be christened in Philadelphia, our last stop before New York. We were sold out for every performance, I was a draw, people wanted to see me. That was a shock, though, a great boost for my morale, since I'd been convinced up to that time that no one would want to see me, no one cared. That had been my perception in Hollywood. George's new scene was terrific, seeming to resolve the major problem. I say "seeming" because how do you resolve the problem when one of two macho men, best friends, dies and returns to earth as a girl who knows she's a man? How do you show Charlie's awakening to awareness as a woman, then have her die again and come back into her friend George's life as a different woman? Well, George Axelrod found a way.

The added scene was almost a monologue for me. And long. We rehearsed it, though we didn't have much time. But it had to go in—so it did. It was a lot to learn—to rethink—breaking away from what I'd been doing for the previous six weeks. I never left the theater that day. All the while I was making up, I was reviewing lines. Sydney came in, and over and over them we went, both nervous as cats. If I forgot a line, the scene wouldn't work. I was in a panic; so was Sydney. But we were actors, and with each performance I had been becoming more of a true professional. There were butterflies in the thousands that night. I was on the edge of a precipice, trying desperately not to fall. Yet I also felt an excitement unlike any I have felt since. It was rebirth. It was my great moment of truth. It was the countdown of spaceship Apollo—my only chance—the final test. Would I survive? I had to!

At last, my entrance. All went well, as all but the end of the play had remained unchanged. Then the new scene was upon us. At the interval between the second and third acts, Sydney and I had gone over the words again. George and Leland came into my dressing room to wish me luck. Not to worry—it would be great. Please God, I said.

My adrenaline was high. As I started the scene, something happened to me that had not happened before. An extra dimension— a creative light—all my juices working: everything fell into place and beyond. The excitement you hope for took over—it was indescribable, and indescribably exciting. The audience reception was fabulous: they sensed something special was happening, and the glory of live theater. I had no idea what I had done or how I had done it. I only knew that it was a thrilling night for me. George and Leland were over the moon, as were we onstage. Sure we had a hit and knowing I had two weeks in Philadelphia to polish my performance.

After eight weeks on the road, the last stop: Broadway. Remember, this was my first time on a Broadway stage, and in a starring part. George insisted we freeze the show at least four performances before closing in Philly. That and a few previews would give us at least a week before the New York opening night. George and Leland went to work on the people placement for the opening. Who sat next to what critic was carefully thought out. Laughers were to be strategically placed. I had had no idea all that went on, but it made perfect sense. I don't know if too many think of it in today's theater, but in a comedy, believe me, the audience had better laugh or you are in trouble. We had one of the grander opening-night audiences. My guests Adlai Stevenson, Alistair Cooke, my mother, bless her (she was always as nervous as I was), plus every bright light on Broadway. I was a wreck. George had told me—told all of us—beforehand, "Just play the play; opening-night audiences in New York are unpredictable. Don't wait for laughs, play the play." An important lesson for all actors for all plays. The opening-night audience of *Goodbye Charlie* reacted peculiarly.

It began with my first entrance and speech of identification. There I was, barefoot in a trench coat, looking like myself, coming off the beach into George's house, where George had just delivered a eulogy at my funeral. A really funny opening scene. Sydney brilliant. Then I came on, convinced George that I was Charlie by sharing with him things only Charlie knew, and proved it by turning my back to the audience and, facing George, opening my raincoat. Shocked, they didn't laugh when they were supposed to. From that moment on, it was downhill with the audience. I didn't know what to think and tried to go on playing the play. Dialogue begins to sound hollow when they don't respond; your voice seems to hang in midair, unprotected, vulnerable. I remember my stomach churning fiercely. Opening night in New York was so different from everyplace else. They had loved us in Philadelphia. Suddenly the reality hits you that your future—everyone's future—depends on this one night. It is terrifying, this plea for acceptance, approval. The need for good reviews. Then, after all the applause, the curtain calls, the cameras, the well-wishers backstage, Leland hosted a small opening-night party at Sardi's.

I distinctly remember standing at the bar with Moss Hart, who told me, "You should feel proud of yourself. Even if this doesn't make it, you have learned that you can do it and that you belong on the stage!" He knew, of course, that it wouldn't make it. As did George, as did Leland. I, on the other hand, did not know. I was a novice at this aspect of theater. I couldn't believe that after the months and months that George had put into writing this play, after all the talents—Leland, Oliver Smith, Mainbocher, the costume designer, and the lighting designer, stage crew, actors—had worked so hard and long, not to mention the money invested, it could be killed in one night. But it could and it was. That, too, is the theater—not the good part. We were sold out for the three and a half months that we played. The movie rights were sold, so at least the investors were paid back.

The critics were cruel to George. They expected—no, demanded—too much of him, could not accept the fact that after his string of hits he might falter or miss. But their cruelty was unnecessary.

And they broke his heart. This talented, intelligent, sensitive, funny, and original man and writer was lost to the theater from then on. That was my first exposure to what an opening night can do to the lives involved—in one night your professional life can be wrapped up, wrung out, and thrown away.

I was left to try to figure out where I had gone wrong. Why hadn't I recognized the play's weaknesses, why hadn't it occurred to me that the play might fail? Blind faith, and I was so deeply involved emotionally that I just assumed it would work. I knew the play had flaws, but the positives far outweighed the negatives. I knew we had a good advance sale, theater parties, so the actual possibility of our closing was not firmly implanted in my brain. I was very preoccupied with the excitement of my first starring part on Broadway.

It was not quite as I had dreamed it when I was sixteen years old—my name in lights and the audience wildly cheering inside the theater as I stood center stage, bowing modestly. At last my name was in lights on a Broadway marquee, but it was not spelled out one bulb at a time, as I had imagined it. And there was no wild cheering. What there was, which I'm not sure I'll ever get used to, is the applause that greeted my first entrance. When Leland and George told me there'd be applause and to wait for it, I didn't quite believe it, nor did I know how I'd react. The applause rises, seems to last forever, I try to start the scene, I speak too soon, thinking the applause will stop. It doesn't, so while I am standing there, trying to keep my attitude and be Charlie in from the sea, I become sixteen-year-old Betty Bacall again and start to shake all over. I am nervous, off balance; I feel naked, exposed, concentration broken. And I *am* exposed, because I am truly inexperienced. And with my concentration broken by the applause, I frankly don't know how to handle it. How I stayed in the theater after going through such agony I'll never know—perhaps I thought the nerves would go away. They haven't. But at least I have learned how to use the opening applause time to advantage.

There is a story told about Gadge Kazan: On opening night he goes backstage and tells all his actors how wonderful they are, to keep up the good work, while in his breast pocket there's an airplane ticket to some faraway land. I don't know if it's true, but it sounds as though it might be—if not of Gadge, then of others. By opening night the director has had enough, he wants to get away. But as an actor, I want him there, dammit. I have to be in that theater six days a week; I've been seeing him all day, every day, for months. I deeply resent being left. I want his support, I need it. Clearly it doesn't work that way. Directors put in their time before a play even starts casting. The actor has to stay sharp and put in his time after it opens. That's his job. It's reasonable. It's the way it is.

Now, as the star of the show I am obliged to set the example of bravery. It is expected. So I try, but it's hard. If I become too miserable, how can I play comedy? Because misery stays behind in the dressing room, or is supposed to. It's a tough profession. The letdown, after eight struggling and hopeful weeks on the road, is monumental. I am sad, so sad! I can't share it with my children; they are too young to understand—God, I don't understand—and they have more than enough to deal with anyway, in a totally new environment, new schools, new home. I don't want to upset my mother, so I cope alone, because I have to. It builds character, they tell me. Through my tears I tell myself this: It will make you strong. You mustn't fall apart.

The last week of the play is the most painful. Having just established a routine, gotten to know the stage crew, made my dressing room home, it has to end. The gradual dismantling of the dressing room filled with personal things that have made me feel permanent. Pictures of my children; a baby pillow for matinee days, when I take a rest or a nap between shows; cards; telegrams taped to my mirror and wall, those opening-night wires full of hope. My own makeup mirror; my makeup, cotton balls, brushes and combs, in their own containers —all so my dressing table looks personal and pleases the eye. I have quickly learned that my dressing room is home for thirty-two or more hours a week, so it must belong to me in every way. Why didn't I know that nothing is permanent? I should have. I had found out that Bogie wasn't.

As each article disappears, it is too painful. I leave as much as I can to the last two days. I don't want to dismantle. I don't want this ending. When this room is empty of all my belongings, where shall I go? My life is a disaster, why did I leave London, do I have any future at all in New York, will I ever work again? Where—when—in what? Every fear I ever had about myself and my life rises to the surface without a moment's hesitation. I work through each one, because I will not let myself collapse, give in. I can't. And I don't work through my anxieties by analyzing. I've lived with one anxiety or another my entire life. I realized a long time ago that I had to pull through. Before Bogie, I had the exuberance of youth to pull me through, and my mother and family for moral support. While Bogie was alive, I had him to boost me, help me through the rough times. After Bogie, I had mostly me and the memory of him. Always my mother. She was my rock, my life-support system. Her confidence in me, her life's experience and instincts, could give me the strength to pick myself up, dust myself off, and start all over again. But it wasn't the same. I wasn't a child anymore. This theater experience was not so long after Bogie, and I was still fragile. So forget self-indulgence, I accepted the way it was—life, that is. I had to, and I had to deal with it one day at a time. Everything seems worse at night and alone. With daylight comes hope for a better day. And on reflection, I'm not as pessimistic as I thought. If I were, I'd have given up years ago. But I will never give up. I refuse to. Isn't hope an incredible, a wonderfully demented thing?

*C*actus *Flower* came six years after *Charlie*. It was a farce, adapted by Abe Burrows from a French play by Pierre Barillet and Jean-Pierre Gredy. With Abe directing and David Merrick producing. I had never played comedy quite like this before. Bordering on farce, it requires tremendous energy and impeccable timing.

A director friend of mine had told me to be sure to have a

movie-out clause in my contract, so I'd be free for a picture he was going to direct, but the only way I could get that was to sign a two-year contract. David Merrick, at the time the most successful producer on Broadway, was a tough taskmaster. Everyone in the theater expected us to be at each other's throats, and were stunned when we weren't.

We rehearsed for three weeks with a small, compact cast: Joe Campanella, the leading man, Brenda Vaccaro, Burt Brincker-hoff, Robert Moore (who would later direct me in *Woman of the Year*). I played a nurse in a dentist's office, Joe being the dentist. Joe had not played comedy before, but he was a good actor, and Abe and David wanted to give him this chance, which was just fine with me. Abe was a brilliant director, playwright, songwriter, collaborator, adapter, you name it. He came to rehearsal full of ideas and sure of what he wanted. I loosened up as we went along, in one scene jumping into the air, legs flying, with Joe on one side and Bob Moore on the other. Abe laughed, so we kept it in. And in this mood, we went to Washington for our first out-of-town opening.

The first view of the set is always exciting. Finding out where the doors are, leading to what rooms, trying not to break your neck as you move in the dark for your quick change. This set was on a turntable, and they can be treacherous. I had a great dresser, Eloise White, a big, happy, fun-loving theater woman. She had always worked with Maureen Stapleton but was free and able to come with me for *Cactus Flower*. A good dresser in the theater is the key to sanity, making life and quick changes bearable. Norman Norell had designed my wardrobe. It was his first outing in the theater, but a great designer is a great designer everywhere, and he was. His major adjustment was zippers—easy, bigger than normal, and long, for quick changes. We went through the tech (lighting), dress rehearsal, photo call, a few previews, and then the opening. As always in Washington, an audience of distinguished politicians and journalists; and a major critic, Richard Coe. I was in my usual state. As nervous for the preview as for the opening. First time in front of an audience. Was it funny? Was I? Would they laugh? And when they were supposed to? I didn't ask myself these questions in order, but they hovered in my head. It turns out that fear has loomed large through most of my professional life, yet each time it's a new experience.

Opening night, my first entrance, applause. Finally, after shakily holding the telephone for what seemed an interminable length of time, I speak my first line. "Dr. Winston's office." Laughter. (Hooray!) Why? Who cares? We're on our way! The show went well, though there were things to fix, as there always are. Some of it didn't work as well as expected, but that's why you go out of town, they say. That's why it's called tryout, they say. That's what it is. With great relief that it's over, I am in my dressing room, getting ready to have a drink, talk to Abe, and then meet some friends. In walks David Merrick, who tells me, "You're a clutch player. You came through with your best performance for the critics. I've just fired Joe Campanella." *What? Why?* "It's not going to work. We took a chance with him, we were wrong, it's hurting the play." I was stunned. I knew there was work to be done, improvements in performance needed, but opening night? Out of town? I'd never heard of that. I did know that Merrick was tough and smart, and that a play and its success was much more important to him than the actors. But this was so cold, so brutal. And there hadn't been a clue. I mean, director and producer are always whispering to each other. In this case, I guess that's what they were whispering about. I went into Joe's dressing room. He, of course, was destroyed. He couldn't believe it, and said, "They didn't even give me a chance. [He was right.] I said, let me play it for a week at least, I'll show you I can do it." But Merrick wouldn't budge. Once his mind was made up, that was it. I felt ghastly for Joe. A perfect way to kill an opening, not to mention an actor.

I looked to Abe, the old pro, the man I counted on and trusted completely for reassurance. When one actor in a company is replaced, all the other actors get nervous. Will one of us be next? That goes for the star as well. Merrick would have done it to me without a moment's hesitation if he decided I wasn't right for the part. Not only was I upset for Joe, but he had to finish out the Washington run,

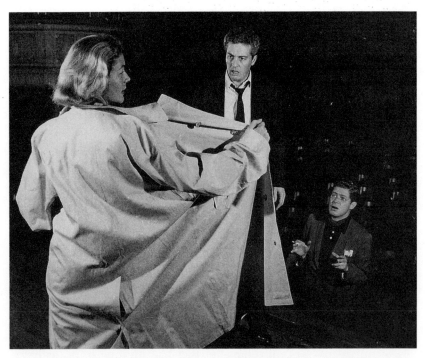

The moment of truth in *Goodbye Charlie*, which unhappily sent a shudder through some of the men in the audience. Sydney's horrified look says it all.

At a New York gathering during the run of *Cactus Flower*, 1967, with Abe Burrows having said or about to say something funny.

which would be tough for us, tougher for him. And who would replace him?

On top of all this, the French playwrights (now my great friends) were witness to what can happen in the American theater. Abe and Merrick were very secretive about a possible successor. They were not sharing their ideas with me, which did not make me happy. I felt I was entitled to hear what they had in mind. But cast approval was not written into that contract, and David was not about to give me anything that was not part of our deal. Another painful example of how certain producers and directors feel about actors. Again, management versus. Meanwhile, I had to perform for the paying public. One night as I was leaving my hotel for the theater, I got a message to stop by the dining room. There was Abe, sitting at a table with Barry Nelson, who was to see the play that night. So that's who they had in mind to replace Joe. There was no time to lose, as we were to open in Philadelphia in less than two weeks. The rehearsals began. Barry was an experienced actor, a good actor, very good at comedy. He had ideas about our scenes and his character that had nothing to do with the present interpretation. His moves were different, blocking had to change. I had fun. It was my first experience seeing two entirely different interpretations of the same part. As Barry found things, so did I. We worked well together. The only catch was that I had to play the play with Barry during the day and play the play with Joe at night. Some of our scenes that were unfunny became unfunnier. I had to remember the old moves while learning the new ones. I became impatient with Joe's work. It wasn't his fault; I just wanted to get on with it. Once I knew he wasn't going to be the Dr. Winston I was going to face eight times a week, something clicked off in my brain. I wanted to work with the Dr. Winston who was going to be permanent. I wanted to improve *my* work, to feel more secure onstage. I was focusing most of my energies into rehearsals with Barry during the day, while trying to maintain enough of an onstage relationship with Joe at night to give a performance. People were still coming and still paying. Some of the time I thought Joe had made the wrong move at the wrong time, because his nighttime moves were not Barry's daytime ones. Plus which, my not-so-beloved father, who lived near Washington, surfaced after more than twenty years. I didn't know when he might be in the audience. Or if he would come backstage. The idea panicked me.

My brain was working overtime. I was so frustrated. I wanted all the laughs that were in the scenes to be realized, I wanted to find new ones, and I couldn't have what I wanted until the change in leading men had been made once and for all. So for ten days I was in hell. Finally the day came. Barry would go on for our last two performances in Washington, so that Philadelphia would be slightly less hysterical, for me at least, as well as for him. I was relieved. At least I could stop being schizophrenic. I said goodbye to Joe, told him how sorry I was that he'd had to go through this, and wished him luck, which I'm happy to say he had.

I had been working so hard, such long hours, I almost lost track of time. So much concentration, focus on only one thing, the play. What a relief to be out of town. It would be impossible to be at home and work like this. Though I always missed home and I definitely missed my children, I was surprised to find myself so completely absorbed in what I was doing that I was almost incapable of thinking of anything else. After a performance, Abe would come into my dressing room with notes; we might go for a drink or a bit of food. During that out-of-town period, and especially with a small cast, you live in each other's pockets. There's little room for an outside life, for the real world. I felt Cactus Flower would be a success, but my judgment on Goodbye Charlie had been so lousy, I was afraid to trust it.

Then suddenly it was opening night in New York. The show turned out to be a big hit. The critics praised me, though they were still not sure I was anything more than a movie star dabbling in the theater.

Every night was like the first night. My heart still pounded, my hands still shook, and I wanted never to be told if anyone I knew or anyone well known was in the audience. No matter how many times I tell myself, "Forget it, stop this foolishness, be a pro, what can they do to you," it doesn't help. If I see a familiar face out front, I am gone—not for long, but gone nonetheless.

At every performance there were standees; the house was completely sold out. Amazing how quickly you get used to that. If there was even one standing-room place unsold, I began to worry. The company manager, of course, reassured me: sometimes weather was the villain, sometimes illness, missed trains or buses; anyway, something quite ordinary and nothing to worry about. I particularly remember one day when it had snowed all the night before and all day. Traffic was at a standstill. People were skiing down Fifth Avenue—no cars allowed—and I was sure we would not be able to play that night; the theater would be empty. I called the stage manager to ask if the show might be canceled. He thought not, so down I went—moving slowly on slippery, snow-covered streets with visibility lousy. What happened? The theater was packed. I don't know how they got there.

Not only was I starring in a smash hit, but I was playing in a theater where I had ushered for many months while dreaming those fifteen-year-old's theatrical dreams. An incredible coincidence in this surprising life. The marquee of the Royale Theater was ablaze with my name and would be for two whole years. There is poetic justice. Unfailingly, several times a week during that run, someone I knew or knew of came to the show. A photograph was taken with each one in my dressing room, and many still adorn my walls. Wonderful memories to keep. So there was often a surprise at the end of the performance, additional excitement, and for me and my great need, approval. It was a happy time. Reinforcement that I had not become an actress in vain.

Time went on, and I still hadn't heard a word about that movie—the movie that I *had* to be free to do. Then I did hear. I heard that the movie was being made, and that the part for which I gave David Merrick an extra year of my life had been cast. I was crushed. My ego took another pounding, and it was a while before I could call my friend the director on it. And all he said when I finally asked him what happened was: "Well, you were in the play." I could have killed him. I wondered when I would stop believing what I was told, counting on promises.

I ended up playing *Cactus Flower* for two solid years, with only one week's vacation at the end of the first year—hardly enough time to rest up for the second. Then to add insult to injury, the movie rights were sold to Columbia Pictures as a vehicle for Walter Matthau, with no guarantee that I would re-create my part for the screen. Here I was in a hit play, having achieved a great personal success, and I still hadn't convinced the Hollywood moguls that I was worth putting in the movie. I was still theoretically auditioning; I still had to prove that I could do it. Is it any wonder that paranoia plays a part in my life? I sink so easily; the scars of childhood remain, the scars of being abandoned, of being unworthy. Much too late in life, I face the fact of permanent damage. No matter how much my mother loved me—and oh, how very much she did—no matter how often she told me I was talented, beautiful, good, one parent can't make up for the one who walked out, no matter how lousy he might have been.

It would soon be June 1967.

Steve, my firstborn, would be graduating from Milton Academy. But it would be more than a graduation, though graduation was enough in itself. It would be Steve, eighteen, venturing out into the big world as an almost adult, having made it through a tough school and having surmounted the growing-up problems that had challenged him emotionally for most of his young life. There was no question I would be there, but it was on a Saturday. Saturday was a matinee day—a two-show day. I would have to explain to David Merrick. He would have to understand. I told my then agent, Peter Witt, that he would have to deal with Merrick. There was no way I was going to miss Steve's graduation. I was his parents. His mother and his father. It was important to both of us that I be there. Peter came back with the word from Mr. Merrick: He would not let me off the hook for that Saturday. Oh God, I thought, a confrontation in the offing. My stomach began tying its series of knots. What kind of man was that? My son was graduating, I was his sole parent. Didn't he understand what that meant?

Again Peter went to Merrick, again he returned: still a definite "no." "I think you'll have to go to his office yourself and speak to him." I hadn't spoken to David Merrick for many months, not since he stormed out of my dressing room one night because I asked him to give my dresser a raise. The request had such an impact on him that he left the theater and refused to speak to me. Nothing would have stopped me from going to Milton Academy for Steve, but I preferred that it be clearly out in the open, with the producer's knowledge, so I finally made an appointment to see him. I went to his office. I'd rehearsed holding myself in: don't explode, be reasonable, pleasant, try not to scream at him, try not to tell him what you really think. And the crawling began. I was, of course, made to wait a few minutes before being ushered into the inner sanctum. At last I was permitted to enter—well-dressed, understated, soft-spoken. The office was dimly lit, very much the same lighting as the room in the Forest Lawn mortuary after Bogie died. Merrick was sitting behind his desk. There was an empty wooden chair for me opposite him, favoring the far corner of his desk. So I sat and started my rehearsed dialogue. "You know why I'm here, David. I don't want a confrontation, I want no unpleasantness. I just want you to understand that my son is graduating from prep school. It is a very important moment for him, for us both, I am his only parent, I must be there." All the time I was talking, I couldn't believe I had to go through this. Was it possible for one human to be so cold, unfeeling, rotten, insensitive? I was proud of my self-control. Of course, I was on the verge of tears, just thinking about Steve's graduating and all those years without Bogie and how proud he would have been of Steve.

After I had spoken, David Merrick came up with his well-thought-out game plan. "Okay, I'll let you go, but just for the graduation; you can only miss the matinee. I will send a car to take you to the airport, a car to meet you in Boston, take you to your son's graduation, then back to Boston, and another car to meet you in New York and bring you straight to the theater. That way you will surely be here for the evening performance. I will not publicize your absence for the matinee, and you are to say nothing about it." Of course, that way no money would be lost. The man was all heart. Also another demonstration of how many producers feel about actors, about stars: the resentment, their need for authority, control. Who's boss. It was Jack Warner all over again. I had no choice but to accept his terms.

Years of so-called stardom had still not given me control of my life. When Jack Warner had advertised *To Have and Have Not* for his theaters all over the country, a photograph of Bogie and me from the movie bore the caption: "Warner employee with girl," Bogie being the employee. That terminology always infuriated Bogie. Actors are *not* employees, yet insofar as we must capitulate to producers we are.

When my two years were finally up, I found myself in California. A meeting had been set up between me and the producer of *Cactus Flower* the movie. I had known him for years, also the director, also Walter Matthau. "I'd love to see you in the movie," the producer said. "But Matthau has the final say, and the director, of course." There was much buck passing. Everyone wanted me, but only one had the final say. After my agent announced at a private dinner, in my presence, that I had been given the part I had created, they cast Ingrid Bergman. That gave me a perfect score: two plays as the original star made into movies with other actresses. Depressing, demoralizing, but that's the business. That's the way it goes, or that's the way it went. Your day will come, I kept telling myself.

About six months after that crushing disappointment, my girlhood dream presented itself. A musical version of Joseph Mankiewicz's *All About Eve* was being thought of; would I be interested? Would I! And how! But could I? Careful now. I met with the composer, Charles Strouse. He wanted to hear me sing. My God! I had always been a frustrated musical performer. I knew the lyrics to almost every song of Gershwin, Porter, Berlin, Kern. I always felt that I would have thrived in speakeasy days, sitting on an upright piano in a smoke-filled room singing those songs. Visual again—dramatic. Singing along late at night and timidly sitting next to a pianist was one thing, but out loud, professionally? My nerves! I'd be terrified to sing for Charles Strouse, however informal he said it would be. I rushed to my voice coach, Keith Davis—who had saved me through my two *Cactus Flower* years—to get at least a few pointers on loosening those vocal cords. That was the beginning of my awareness of what was involved in preparing for a musical comedy. Once everything was in place and director-choreographer Ron Field set (Ron, a choreographer, was to direct for the first time), I started to train. Six months before casting began, I started working on my body with Ron and his assistant. For the dancing part, meeting in a dance studio, learning dancers' warm-up routines, some modern jazz choreography, stretching, barre (back to my childhood ballet days). Every day for two hours, plus a daily voice lesson, breathing exercises. Then after my voice lesson, I'd work on songs with Peter Howard, an ace conductor, pianist, musician. Songs in general and then specifically on the two or three Charles and Lee Adams had already written for the show. All this to build stamina, get my frame in shape, and learn how to do it all so it would be second nature. Second nature was the key. To breathe while singing so no one would notice. And to move in the context of jazz dancing, though not with Fred Astaire, as I had once dreamed.

Each day I would feel new pains, from muscles I didn't even know were there. Every limb had to learn that it was okay to go in the opposite direction of nature's intention. Every section of my body had to learn to move in ways it never had before. Epsom salts found their way into my nightly bath. I learned some control. I came closer to a dancer's life—it's the body, it's the care and feeding of the body, it's keeping legs warm with leg warmers, breaking in your ballet shoes, your jazz shoes, it's doing everything and anything to prevent, or try to prevent, damage. Once a muscle is pulled, a cartilage torn, your job is in jeopardy. All of the above is also true of the voice, the instrument that is an actor's life. There is no life without it. And the energy required, the energy expended, is indescribable. I've always been long on energy, and it has served me well, but there were times during rehearsal when I wondered if I'd make it.

Music feeds me, gives me life. It always has. When it came to rehearsing musical numbers, I was always buoyed up by the sound of those notes and the fact that I was dancing with the gypsies, not alone. The first time we ran through the first few scenes, the people not in them sat around and watched. I remember them staring at me, my added self-consciousness because of that, my wondering was I good enough. Life without confidence is tough indeed. If I found it so challenging to dance in front of the company, how would I ever be able to sing in front of them—or anyone? I at least knew that I could move. I had studied dance for thirteen years; I was graceful. But to sing for the composer, who wanted to hear a beautiful voice and instead heard mine? I had to overcome these fears. I had to bluff my way through.

I'm a worker. I'm fully aware that acting onstage is not done with mirrors, but I hadn't a clue about the kind of preparation necessary for a musical. And all this before rehearsals began. But I had a goal. To see if I could do this without falling on my face, ending my erratic career; to be terrific while playing a part originated by Bette Davis, my childhood idol. Her performance was definitive, perfect, and will remain so forever. But that's okay; I'd taken it on on the basis that this was not the same thing—it was a musical; otherwise I wouldn't have dared. And I wanted to prove to myself that I was capable of doing it. I had to find out.

I wanted to be as ready as I could be by the time we went into rehearsal. Once I started to prepare, my focus hour by hour was on that. I became conscious of every breath I took and move I made when I wasn't actually in a class. This preparation gradually consumed me. Going to Europe for my last holiday for at least a year and a half, I took Leslie and Sam to David Niven's in Cap-Ferrat, laden with tapes of the songs I was to learn, vocal exercises I was to practice daily. I would sit on the point of Cap-Ferrat in my bathing suit, vocalizing loud and clear, then try to sing the songs. David said I sounded like a seal calling for its mate. Fortunately, I was not listening.

Back in New York, we had a reading of the play at Ron's house, authors and composers present. The first meeting of actors who were going to work together for a long time to come, God and *The New York Times* willing. Followed by eight weeks of rehearsal—two on the dances, the rest on book and songs. A lot of hard, concentrated work, plus getting a feel for your fellow players. Along with the others, I was quite self-conscious at first, then I had to rise above who and what the rest of the company thought I was. The gypsies wanted to see if I was a regular girl or if I would be snobbish, difficult. Then it turned out that some of the actors were slightly in awe of me. Now, I know that I do not inspire awe, but my association with Bogie does, so there was that to deal with. Others were determined to treat me as just another actress, with some succeeding better than others. The main problem for me was that they all came in with their minds made up. They had their preconceived notions. All the result of years of magazine, and newspaper hype, plus rumors, most of it fiction. So I was auditioning again.

Musicals require boldness. Acting requires boldness. Laying your life on the line eight times a week is not for the meek and mild. The performer I admired most on the musical stage, the one whose attitude I aspired to, was Ethel Merman. Walk out on that stage as if you own it, stand straight, feet apart, sure. I once saw her pre-Broadway time and told her I was nervous. "Nervous?" she said. "Why are you nervous? If they could do what you do, they'd be onstage and you out front." She was absolutely right; all I had to do was convince myself.

I remember how I felt during our first run-through for the producers, authors, composers. The writers who had adapted Mankiewicz's *All About Eve* were Betty Comden and Adolph Green, two of my dearest friends. Just try to envision a large rehearsal hall, mirrors on one wall (where there are dancers, there are always mirrors, and our rehearsal hall was a dance studio—Eliot Feld's, in actual fact). Terrible metal folding chairs line the wall, a table off to one side holds all the director's and the stage manager's equipment, a piano's on the other side of the room. The jury—producers Joe Kipness and Larry Kasha; Comden and Green; Charles Strouse and Lee Adams—on those folding chairs against the wall, and all the performers on the other side of the floor tape representing the stage. So right off the bat it is made clear: actors versus management. We were going to be judged. Even though theater is a cooperative effort, even though you love one another, it is still actors on one side, management on the other. There weren't butterflies in my stomach; that would be too tame. Armies—marching armies of soldier ants would be more like it. I felt a constant rumbling. Terror had struck.

The room is brightly lit, so all faces are very clearly seen. The only mood created comes from the play, from us hoping not to be shot down. I start concentrating very hard, trying to eliminate from my brain that "they" are there. So what if they are. I am Margo Channing, I know her well, and we on our side of the tape are together. We have lived together for all these weeks and have months to go, and what we share "they" can never be part of, it belongs to us exclusively. I go through this monologue, and as the imaginary curtain rises and I begin to speak, the nerves remain but they gradually move into the body of Margo Channing and, except for an occasional lapse, stay there.

The thrill of getting through it the first time. The excitement I felt did not allow me to think in terms of good or bad. I just knew I was doing it and loving it and loving everything connected with it. I had then, and still sometimes have, a terrible habit: every time I make a mistake, blow a line, I stop dead, my mind a blank, so preoccupied with the line missed that I mess up the ones that follow. In spite of the fact that I fell victim to that bad habit once or twice, the authors were smiling at the end of the run-through. They were happy. There was still work to be done, but they liked us—my friends were pleased with me. I had passed the musical test for Betty and Adolph. I could do it!

My private life came to a dead stop from the day I started rehearsal. I wasn't giving up anything, really: my mother had died, I'd gotten a divorce, Steve was married. There were Leslie and Sam at home with me. We'd have dinner together, many hugs and kisses, but children do go on with their lives. If you don't join them, they move along just the same. Lucky for them that they do. I was grateful not to be sharing my life with anyone but them.

Before we left for our first out-of-town stop, Baltimore, Ron decided we should have a gypsy run-through. That is an experience unlike any other. It usually takes place in the afternoon, on a non-matinee day. Gypsies and casts from other shows are invited, plus directors, producers, composers—show folk. It was to be held at the Lunt-Fontanne Theater. No sets, no costumes, no orchestra, just us chickens and a piano. It sounded like more torture to me, but then everything did, everything was. I'd made up my mind that I would get through anything that I had to to succeed in the musical theater. Torture was an accepted factor? So be it. They were an overboard audience. The best part to me was that they were out front and we were onstage, where they couldn't get at us. Ron started the afternoon

Me living out my musical dream in *Applause* at the Palace Theater, 1970.

explaining the set, the time, the year, then the nonexistent curtain rose. The soldier ants were fighting with the butterflies, and the ants were winning. I was on such a high, though—the exhilaration was wonderful, truly wonderful. Not only that I worked my way through my nerves and was able to perform, to sing and dance, and with only a piano, but that I felt pretty damn good doing it. And the extraordinary thing was that I absolutely felt that I belonged in a musical. The sense of joy I felt in *Applause* was unique. That particular musical was clearly a case of a perfect marriage. The Margo Channing of *Applause* and myself were ideally suited. She was approaching middle age; so was I. She was insecure; so was I. She was being forced to face the fact that her career would have to move into another phase as younger women came along to play younger parts; so was I. And she constantly felt that the man she was in love with was going to go off with someone else, of course someone younger, and I, too, had had those feelings. So Margo and I had a great deal in common.

I understood, I connected with her problems, her frailties, even her slight paranoia. With each role one searches for understanding, and always you have to be willing to dig deeply into your own life to find that connection and identification. The more I played Margo Channing, the more united we became. As I approached each scene in which Margo became vulnerable through her insecurity and fought against showing it, I realized how acute my own was. Finally, after playing the part for a year, heading into the second, it was sometimes difficult for me to see where she left off and I began. I became a woman alone in life and an actress alone onstage, so in a weird way I was alone twice as much as I would have been had I not been playing Margo Channing. Ron Field had staged my curtain call at the end of the show in a way I had never seen—or have seen since, I might add. I stood far up center stage with my back to the audience. The entire company had taken their calls and were standing in a V formation, arms outstretched toward me at the apex of the V. On cue I whirled around, arms out and up, and headed downstage to music and the audience's wild applause. *Applause* music. The audience hadn't known where I was coming from for my bow, so the lift it gave them, plus the lift the audience gave me, plus the music, was like the thrill of the high point of a political convention and more. When Jean Negulesco came backstage after the show to congratulate me, he said, "You don't need a man in your life; you have this. No man can ever give you what this show gives you." I never forgot that. I knew what he meant. There's nothing like it: the excitement of a hit, the roar of applause, the music, the tremendous affirmation and love that comes across the footlights, are hard to equal. But why couldn't I have both? I thought. Why was that impossible?

By the time I had rehearsed and played *Applause* in New York, on a national tour, and in London, it had consumed almost five years of my life, and I had out-Margoed Margo. She had permeated my life to such an alarming degree that her words often became my words. In my final scene, when I told my friend Karen how at last I knew that nothing had much meaning unless you could look across the table at someone, reach toward someone in bed, knowing that he understood you and shared with you and loved you, it might have been me. A revelatory scene. Not a new idea but a potent one, basic and true. Love *is* what matters. Playing that scene, I was always on the brink of tears, as it was brought home to me that it *was* true, and that love was something I did not have.

It took a long time for me to recover from that emotional drainage. While I have always prided myself on being truthful, knowing my faults and personal problems, it is quite another thing to face yourself in front of an audience eight times a week for five years. A relentless exercise. I worked my way through my own misery enough to continue to perform. Not an easy task, but no one ever said it would be easy.

At the end of the London run of *Applause*, after an unhappy love affair had ended, I felt that it was almost me, myself, confessing to the audience, the audience of strangers. That really was baring my soul, and I had to stop in order to survive. I had to do something different, see something different, shake myself and my life into a fresh outlook. A new beginning.

I got lucky. *Murder on the Orient Express* came along. A

movie. What a great break for me! I was again playing an actress, but this time not an actress with Margo Channing problems: no man involved, no frustrated love, this time just a grown-up woman in a murder plot. The company was filled with old friends—John Gielgud, Rachel Roberts, Sidney Lumet directing—and new friends, Wendy Hiller, Albert Finney, Jean-Pierre Cassel, Sean Connery, Ingrid Bergman. It was such a happy experience. My good friend Tony Walton designed superb costumes, as well as reproducing the train to the minutest detail. The movie saved me, it broke my theater rhythm.

After ten years away from a movie set, it was almost like starting again. And watching John Gielgud, Wendy Hiller, Albert Finney work, I was learning more. I'd forgotten how much I enjoyed making movies. It was fresh, exciting, and—that hated word—challenging. Wonderful actors create an aura, they enter a room with it. John, of course, is a great actor and, like most great actors—there aren't many—he makes it look easy. He also makes everyone who works with him better.

As I have worked more, moving between theater and film, I have found that one day, for no specific reason, I have arrived at a better place. More secure in what I do—surer. I suppose it comes from practice, awareness, knowing more, and getting older. It's a very good feeling indeed.

It's very odd, but it seems to me that my great successes onstage have always come at a turning point in my life. Never planned—just happened. In a way, the theater has saved me. Which was pure, unadulterated luck, plus my willingness to jump.

*Cactus Flower*, when I was sitting in California, getting no movie offers, was the beginning of almost twenty years of four positive experiences for me. And I wasn't particularly looking for anything onstage. It was fated.

*Applause* came during another struggling period in my career—and when my marriage was failing and my mother's health deteriorating. A completely depressing period.

*Woman of the Year* arrived when I was again treading water, trying to stay afloat. No movie offers—the theater once again renewed me. And not long after that, when I needed it, along came more than I ever dreamed of for me: *Sweet Bird of Youth*.

One day back in New York, late in the fall of '84, my agent called to tell me that Duncan Weldon, an important London theatrical producer, wanted to know if I would be interested in coming to London to play in Tennessee Williams's *Sweet Bird of Youth*. First I was flattered, then I was thrilled, then, on reading the play, I became excited and then scared, and *then* I started thinking. Who could direct? After the playwright, the director was the key.

Alexandra del Lago is an actress, a princess, a great star whose career is somewhat on the brink. It is all-important to her, and the fear of its ending leads her to fill her time with drink, drugs, and sex—anything to forget the possible nothingness that lies ahead. I had never been in a play that was written by a poet, and the prospect filled me with wonder. What would it be like? I could hardly wait to find out. The fear in Alexandra del Lago was not unlike the fear in Margo Channing, though Alexandra had more grandeur and was more dramatic and crazed. Her first sounds in the opening scene were moans followed by screams. Screaming had never been my forte, so I was a little intimidated. My voice was/is not a screaming voice. But then I said to myself, "You have to forget all that, get into the skin of this woman, and the scream will be fine." I had the greatest piece of luck any actress could have when Harold Pinter agreed with enthusiasm to direct.

I was stimulated by the words of Tennessee, by the torment of him and his people. Gradually I found myself inhabiting his world.

*Sweet Bird of Youth*, London, 1985: Alexandra del Lago's moment of realization that her movie is a hit! She is queen once again.

Again *Sweet Bird*, with Chance Wayne forcing the princess to face herself.
She remains in control and triumphant.

With a playwright like Williams, there is no way to avoid it. Once again, the fear of a futureless future rose to the surface. Onstage I lived so many of the Princess's fears, they were intertwined with my own. At times during rehearsal I thought, Oh God, here I go again, exposing myself, all my apprehensions, saying it all out loud. Now everyone will know. That's what acting is. Parts like that can make you slightly schizophrenic. As over and over again I talked about the passage of time, it cut me; when I had to look in the mirror onstage, as I had to fairly often, I could see that enemy on my face, I could feel it in my body. If I faltered, I was her, I was me. Yet I was not her: I have never given in to drugs, liquor, or men in order to forget. It doesn't work anyway; it didn't for the Princess. That kind of forgetting does not last very long. The past is always there.

Alexandra del Lago lived from role to role. Stardom was her hero and her mate, she needed adulation, admiration—success, affirmation—everything that stardom brings with it. When I started to play her, I was living alone in London, with my three children in America. I could relate to the Princess. I was less manic, less extreme, but as I went along night after night, the weeks growing to months, I made many discoveries. With a writer like Tennessee Williams, there are always endless layers to his characters. So discovery is a constant. For example, in the beginning of the play, she seems—she *is*—desperately in need of Chance Wayne, not only for sex but so as not to be left alone, not to be left alone to think and to face what she considers to be her fading or finished career, her age, her empty, lonely life. As the story unfolds, the changes begin and the interactions of the characters take many directions. There are always unexpected moments in a play when you suddenly find something new in your part, do something different in a scene. It's unexplainable and unpredictable: the moment is always so fleeting I seldom can pinpoint it or even remember or define it. It just happens. In the last scene of the play, Chance places a phone call to the all-powerful Hollywood columnist Sally Powers, desperately wanting Alexandra to tell her she has found a new young star (his fantasy) in Chance.

This is the call Alexandra has dreaded, for it will tell her that her just-released movie is a disaster and her career all but over. Instead, as the conversation with Sally Powers continues, she discovers that her reviews were brilliant, that she is once again a smashing success. In that instant the Princess reveals her strength—she becomes sure of herself, she grows two inches taller with self-confidence and joy. She forgets Chance Wayne; she doesn't need him now. She can return to Hollywood, head held high; they will cheer her, she will be adored, she is once again the great star she always was. So she has staved off her career's demise one more time.

As the run of the play wore on, each time I approached that scene, all of the emotions of fear, anticipation, the internecine war of wanting and not wanting, combined in me, and as my conversation with Sally progressed, my stomach would tighten, my back would straighten; my immediate future became clear and exciting. I felt such exhilaration, had such a sense of power. And of course I came to discover how I myself needed to have those feelings. How much better I always felt the minute I knew I had a role to play. Even now I get more pleasure out of leisure when I know there's a job waiting in the wings. So the Princess and I came together at the end of the play. An amazing feeling. An incredible high. A catharsis.

In this play with its extraordinary and poetic language, I found that as I spoke, the words surrounded me, made me warm and safe, held me up. That kind of writing does almost all the work, and Tennessee was one of the few playwrights in my lifetime who could provide it. He made me feel that I was a better actress. I could be reckless, could let go, I could rise to his occasion. And if not—I could come close. Closer than I ever had before.

I played Alexandra del Lago for over six months in England, followed by four and a half in Australia, where I was the only non-Australian in the production. Colin Friels, a marvelous actor, played Chance Wayne, and brilliant he was. It was quite an experience for me to first play with an English cast (except for the American Michael Beck's superb Chance Wayne) in a country that has been a second home to me and then to follow with an Australian cast in a

With Tennessee Williams backstage at
*Cactus Flower*, 1967.

Rehearsal before opening in Bath, with Harold
Pinter—one of my greatest theatrical experiences.
Harold as one great playwright leading me through
the scenes of another great playwright.

country I barely knew. Good actors are good actors everywhere, and I was lucky on both occasions. But England and Australia are very different cultures. In Australia I had to adjust, in spite of my reluctance to change too much in my performance. We had the same set, the same overall production as in England, but I obviously couldn't give the same performance with Colin Friels as with Michael Beck. I think I was better in Australia. I hope I was; I should have been. I was still learning to open up more, to take more time. But I see now how much better I could have been. Always can be. Yet how lucky I was to have this second time around, this opportunity to alter my choices and add to my performance.

The experience of *Sweet Bird of Youth* was worth everything. I would hate to think that I will never be in a play as worthy again. I certainly counted my blessings to be in that one. At the end of the Australian tour I had played Alexandra del Lago eight times a week for over a year and was ready for a break in rhythm. I wanted to return to the making of movies. Easier said. But I'm a nervy gal, and I'd made up my mind. I was going to reacquaint myself with that world once more, and I did. The parts have been far from staggering, but I've worked and kept on working. So that's something.

It may be wishful thinking, but I have the sense that good things are waiting just around the corner. At this point it has been six years since the last curtain rang down for me on a stage. I've been working steadily in film these last few years, and as work usually leads to more work—who knows? A little bit of luck could be heading my way. The great thing now is that there are more choices than ever before. I've added lecturing to my agenda. Yet I have an itch to be onstage once more—in an original play, preferably. Revivals are fine if they're classics, but otherwise no. There I go again, making rules when there aren't any.

Not very long ago I completed a movie with Gregory Peck for Turner Television. We had worked together thirty-six years before in *Designing Woman*, and worked well. But for no reason at all, there'd been nothing more until *The Portrait* two years ago.

We had played a married couple in *Designing Woman* and once again a married couple in *The Portrait* (married for over thirty years). Greg and I always liked each other—felt much the same way about the world and our profession. In the thirty-six-year interim we had gone on with our lives and our work, and we brought those life experiences with us last year. We shared a daughter in *The Portrait*— Greg's real-life daughter. My younger son was almost the same age as she. It seemed the most natural thing in the world to work together again—in a way, living out our lives again—bringing those past years with us, understanding the changes in both of us and what we had experienced. It was a great gift.

And to follow that—wonder of wonders—along came *A Foreign Field*, a BBC movie for television, with Alec Guinness, Jeanne Moreau, Leo McKern, Geraldine Chaplin, Ed Herrmann, and John Randolph, directed by Charles Sturridge of *Brideshead Revisited*. What a break! To work with those people—Guinness, Moreau. I was thrilled, excited, and naturally nervous. It was filmed in Normandy and London—what could be better? The answer is: nothing. We all lived in a grand château and dined together nightly. I had to pinch myself to be sure it was really happening. It was!

All that I started with—enthusiasm, hope, curiosity, anxiety, ambition—all remain. My profession still excites me, though the business of it doesn't. I feel nothing that even vaguely resembles complacency. I still look forward to the discovery of the unknown. I still feel the need for self-expression, the need to become someone else —and the need to hide. The need to dream. That great sense of health and accomplishment and fun that work gives can be compared to nothing on this earth. It will never be everything to me, but it comes close.

# FRIENDSHIP
# AND LOSS

In the world of relationships, possibly the most complicated, uncommon, hard to find, hard to keep, and most rewarding has got to be friendship. I speak as a woman whose life to a large degree has centered on and depended on friends—one whose feeling of belonging has come from the continuity of friendship. As I reflect on my life, I see that from the not so advanced age of twenty on, it is friends that have been the continuing thread—my connection with where I am, with where I have been, where I am going; my need, sometimes my cushion, sometimes my confidante. They have made me laugh, moved me to tears, hurt me, helped me, changed me. Extraordinary that I have been so lucky.

Having had a life with a man twenty-five years my senior, I was able to have friends of his generation: wonderful writers like Louis Bromfield and John O'Hara; wits and originals like Noël Coward, Nunnally Johnson, Robert Benchley; Spencer Tracy; journalists like Quentin Reynolds; characters like Irving Lazar and, in the music world, Ira Gershwin. Then there was the next generation: John Huston, David Niven, Alistair Cooke, Richard Brooks, Katharine Hepburn . . . segueing to Adolph Green, Leonard Bernstein, Betty Comden, Arthur and Alexandra Schlesinger, to arrive closer to my contemporaries Phyllis Newman, Gen Leroy, Tony Walton, Roddy McDowall, Jean Smith, Joan Axelrod, and on and on . . . and that's only in America. And it's not half of those who have given me so much, have added so much to my knowledge, appreciation, different point of view. I couldn't have made it through my life without them. And without their significant others, who were in almost all cases very significant to me as well.

Because I travel so much to work, I have become more aware of the changes in friendships. I somehow always thought they would never change—I expected them not to, I hoped they wouldn't. But people do change, lives change, and with that, I suppose, friendships must.

I seem to be spending more and more time in Paris and in London—the friendships there have become stronger, and new friendships have been fostered and fed because I am there. Why I am continually surprised by the slight schism that occurs with absence, I'm not quite sure. My guess is that it has a lot to do with my not being a couple, my need being greater than theirs, my not having an other, significant or otherwise, to share with, bounce off, beef to. And if sometimes there's more enthusiasm from my French and British friends, I charge that to the fact that I'm not there long enough for them to tire of me. Also I'm as happy to be there as they are to have me there.

There are so many kinds of friendship: those from childhood and school; friendships—the passing friendships, the faraway ones; the I-would-do-anything-for-you, the understanding, compassionate; the part-time social and the work friendships. Except for the from-childhood ones, I would guess I've had, and do have, them all. For me, there is still nothing to compare with the sound of a familiar voice filled with warmth and welcome when I pick up a phone.

As I have spent so many years alone, I cannot imagine what

might have happened to me without friends—people with whom I have shared so much of my life, erratic and sad though some of these friendships have been. I want them to have health and wealth and to live forever. As the number has shrunk, as the gaping holes multiply —as pieces of me go with those who leave this earth—I become more aware of my own mortality and the incredible sadness that endings bring.

At a memorial service for a departed friend, words, experiences, even laughter, mingle with tears and are shared. It's after that that the real gnaw begins: the day in, day out knowledge that that particular voice—that special connection, that unspoken commitment, the thread that tied you together—is broken, gone, that you will never see that face or hear that voice again. You never get used to it. The old saw that time heals all wounds doesn't quite wash. Time helps—it's the only thing that does; it helps you to go on, to live, to laugh, to love—but it doesn't help you to forget or lessen the tiny stab of pain that remembrance brings.

Mildred. When we first met I was nineteen, she somewhere in her late thirties. She was the wife of Bogie's agent and friend, Sam Jaffe, and she was beautiful, beautiful in a totally unstereotypical Hollywood way. Long, dark hair parted in the middle and worn in a bun; clear-blue, deep-set eyes; generous mouth; high cheekbones. She was biblical-looking, with a strong face that reflected her love and appreciation of art. In the beginning I thought of Mildred and Sam as Bogie's friends, and as time went on I thought of them as ours: good, mutually simpatico, but not intimate. Gradually, with the birth of my first child, Stephen, Mildred and I grew closer.

She gave me my first taste of art. For our first Christmas, the Jaffes sent us a Toulouse-Lautrec poster, and so began my awareness. I knew nothing of art, a kid who grew up in New York with a

Mildred when first I met her: beautiful, witty, loving, and giving.

working mother who had terrific taste and no money—no matter how small, where we lived was always cozy, attractive—and whose long work hours deprived her of time to look for little treasures or to teach a restless teenage aspiring-actress daughter. Or, for that matter, to learn herself. My preoccupation was with the performing arts. Hers, to see that I got what I wanted.

It was through Mildred, the houses she made, the antiques she filled them with, the pictures she lived with, that I became aware of artists' names and their work. She had tremendous curiosity and enthusiasm. She loved the young, the talented, the undiscovered. She did not follow the crowd. She was a Jewish mother, passionate about her husband and her three daughters. Passionate about her friends, their lives. She loved introducing me to new things, glowed if I was responsive. And she was an original, a lover of the Impressionists but also a great lover of Mexican art, of all things Indian and African. She introduced me to all these cultures. I was too busy with my new life of wifedom and motherhood to absorb it all. It took me longer than I had wished, but my art education had begun.

In 1952, the presidential campaigns were about to begin. There was Eisenhower on the Republican side and an unknown named Adlai Stevenson on the Democratic side. I, a lifelong Democrat, favored Eisenhower and for not very profound reasons, except that President Truman had tried to entice him into being the Democratic candidate. That was good enough for me, that plus his war record and his irresistible smile, and I had not seen or heard Stevenson as yet. I had just given birth to Leslie. Mildred came to visit, carrying with her a book by John Bartlow Martin about Adlai Stevenson, governor of Illinois. "Read it before you make your decision," she said. "Read it and you'll change your mind." I read it, watched Stevenson making his acceptance speech at the convention, and fell hook, line and sinker. From that moment on, Ike was out and I became a devoted follower of and worker for Adlai. Funny that despite the disparity in our ages, Mildred and I were completely in harmony.

The Jewish background is a strong bond. We both had it, though I was less religious than she. She acted both as a contemporary of mine and as my California mother. Without really being aware of it, I found myself depending on her for advice. When Bogie and I were going to do the living room in our new house, she introduced me to her decorator, who was a great decorator but turned out to be a kleptomaniac. I only half thanked Mildred for that one. Only once did she falter, and it wasn't in friendship. She came to visit Bogie when he was very ill; she hadn't seen him for a few weeks, and she gasped at the sight of him. She hadn't expected the change. I understood, but I told her she could never come to the house again if she could not control or disguise her feelings. She accepted the scolding and handled herself impeccably from then on.

She was an emotional woman, she loved Bogie, it was hard for her. After he died, she kept close watch on me. I could talk to her about him; she had known him so long and so well. She would commiserate with me as my own mother would, except that it was easier for me with Mildred because I didn't want to upset or worry my mother, and besides, my mother was in New York.

I was leaving California, going to London for almost a year to make a movie, taking my children. Before I left, Mildred took me to see a man who had brought some small sculptures over from England. He was a private art dealer. I saw the sculptures, and one in particular really affected me. I had a physical reaction to it that I had never felt from paintings. It was small, a bronze maquette of a reclining woman. The sculptor was Henry Moore. I had not heard of him then, but from that moment on he became a part of my life.

When my mother had her first heart attack, Mildred was immediately on the phone. It happened in New York, fortunately when I was there. Mildred was there for me during my crisis, to do whatever was needed, to provide solace. But the great thing about her was that she was there for me when there was no crisis. She was there every day, night and day, in the same total, giving way. She was there at the unimportant times, at the times when I most needed a special friend.

And fun—she was always fun. She and Sam had moved to England years before I went there for two years. I lived a few blocks away, so we were together a lot, and when we weren't together the phone would ring. I'd pick it up and hear "Nu?" Mildred wanting to know my plans for the day, did I want to go to a gallery, look at some art, there was a young artist whose work was interesting, worth seeing.

Mildred loved color, purple being favored. Her bedroom was in the palest lavender, with chairs, a table, a small chest, a clock in black papier-mâché. The woman had flair. And taste, curiosity, and wisdom. Considering the fact that she was a nonworking woman, actually in the housewife category, she was a freer, more independent spirit than many of today's feminists are. She was not one to live in the kitchen, to go to lunch. She was a doer, an involved person, a partaker of life. I've never known anyone remotely like her.

After more than fifteen years in London, Sam announced

that they were returning to California to be near their children. Mildred didn't want to go, but she deferred to her husband of fifty years. They tried La Jolla for a while, but for all its loveliness, after a few strolls on the beach she was ready for the loony bin. She needed people, she needed stimulation.

One day she called to tell me that Sam had cancer of the jaw and would need surgery and radiation. He was over eighty years old. She was terribly worried and upset, but she hung in there, of course, and went every step of the way with him. Then a couple of years later, by some devastating twist of fate, she came down with it. Ovarian cancer. She had had some pain, but true to Mildred she had never mentioned it.

After surgery she needed chemotherapy. She was most worried about her hair. She had kept it black and long for all of her seventy-six years. What would happen now? We were in constant touch; I hated being so far away. She was doing well. As I said to Sam, "You have done everything together, now this too, and she will recover as you have!" When I got to L.A., she was wearing stylish knitted skullcaps. She came to my hotel room, took off the cap at my behest, and there was a small covering of gray hair on her scalp. She looked more beautiful than ever. It was no ordinary gray, mind you, it wouldn't dare to be; for Mildred, it was silver. She was not melodramatic about her condition. All she said was: "I've had a good life, a happy life. I have no complaints. Now tell me about your life: are you alone, how are the children, what is your work story?"

My young son, Sam, had been married in May, and he and his wife had given me a book of their wedding photographs. Mildred was anxious to see them. By that time she had gone through a second course of chemotherapy and had lost all her hair; the prognosis was negative. She was tired most of the time and was spending a great deal of time in bed. I brought her the book, sat on the bed with her, and as I turned the pages, pointing out who was who in the photographs, her concentration ebbed. You know, homes change drastically when illness comes through the door. There is a sense of emptiness and terrible sadness that permeates the entire abode. And it's the light—that's what I have noticed most. With health, all rooms are operational—all lamps are lit. With illness, it's just the living room for friends—and the bedroom for the one who's the center of it all, and the light is never bright. And through the entire home there is a silence, almost a hospital silence. Without defining it, instinctively you speak softly. For the joy has gone. It all became very clear one particular afternoon when I was visiting her and she made the effort to sit in the living room for about an hour. We were trying to talk in generalities—people we knew, what I was doing. As we walked back to her bedroom, she said, "I am not of this world."

So she knew. She had no interest anymore in the present or the future. She wanted to be with her family. I was one of the privileged few, as the fourth daughter who could come at any time. She never had to put on a show for me. To watch this beautiful, vital woman fade away was like losing a part of me. When I saw that she had lost interest in almost everything around her, I knew that she would die. I was in despair. I had grown up with her. She had shown me the distaff side of movie and California life. She had demonstrated the necessity for interest in things outside the industry and the continuance of grace in the face of it. I stayed in California to spend time with her. Finally I had to return home, but I called and spoke with Sam constantly. And one day, not long after I'd left, my phone rang. She was gone. I mourned; I had lost my second mother, my dear, darling friend. There would not be another like Mildred. Not for me.

I could never comprehend her sixty-year marriage to Sam. How do people stay together that long? Who gives up what? Bogie and I were married for eleven and a half years, Jason and I for eight. Being a product of divorce, I had never thought a relationship could last beyond five years. The Jaffes' mutual love of family, their shared Judaism, their respect for each other, I suppose those are the things that kept them together. They had rocky times like anyone else, but they stayed together. There have to be times when one or the other

Sam and Mildred close here as they were for more than sixty years.
There are many lifetimes in these eyes.

wants to take off, get away, see a new face, have a fresh experience. I'm sure there were such times with Sam and Mildred. But something was strong enough to keep them from doing that. They were lucky. They loved each other.

And Mildred lives with me daily on my fireplace mantel with its Henry Moore sculptures—the first one center stage—through my African figures on my walls. Wherever I roam she lives throughout my house. Her glorious gift to me. And that part of my heart that was hers she will forever own.

E ndings. How I hate them, how painful they are. Each time a friend dies, the present becomes the past, in an instant. When Laurence Olivier died, I thought of the first time we met: 1950. So many years ago, yet the picture remains crystal clear. An event: the Oliviers, Laurence Olivier and Vivien Leigh, were coming to Beverly Hills. Danny and Sylvia Kaye were giving a welcoming party at the ballroom of the Beverly Hills Hotel. It was the party to make all other parties look sick. Every movie star anyone ever heard of, every top director and studio head, all Hollywood was there, and I mean all. I've never seen anything like it before or since. Royalty could not have had a more lavish welcome. And Larry and Vivien were theatrical royalty, so the event was fitting. Bogie and Larry and Vivien and I clicked immediately. She was warm, open, loved to laugh, was incredibly easy and ravishingly beautiful. Larry and Bogie shared Noël Coward and Clifton Webb as old friends, enjoyed drinking and talking theater together. I was somewhat in awe of Larry—well, not somewhat, very much in awe. I watched and listened a good deal at all gatherings for them, and there were many. Larry loved to clown. He and Bogie shared drinks and hats at a Sunday lunch that lasted all day at Clifton Webb's house. It was a high time. A great time. A vanished time. Canasta was the rage then, and Vivien and I would play at George Cukor's house. That visit of theirs was golden, and it began a friendship that lasted until their deaths. Bogie and I were heading for our first trip to London, Paris, Rome, and then Africa for the making of *The African Queen*. Larry and Vivien would be in London when we arrived; they gave us places to go and special places to stay as we drove through the south of France. Vivien loved France, had to go at least once a year for her spirit. I now understand that need—though once a year would never do it for me.

They were a magical couple, strictly fairy-tale time. Both beautiful, both talented, smart, funny. Larry was harder to get to know, a man of many complexities. Vivien, too, was complicated, more so than I realized at the beginning, but she was more of a social animal. She gave herself to a friendship immediately, she did with me, and that of course made her irresistible. Larry had a calling. Most of his friendships stemmed from work, from mutual creativity, so it took him longer to open up on a pure interacting level. It was years before I felt close to him.

In 1953 I was in Palm Springs for a weekend. On checking into my hotel, I was handed three messages from Vivien, saying that she was on her way down and would call on arrival; she was most anxious to get in touch with me. That was the last I heard, but on returning to town I went to a dinner party and there she was. She said she had tried many times to reach me and had finally given up, though actually she never got to Palm Springs. Her behavior was just a little odd.

A few nights later, Charlie Feldman gave a very small dinner at Don the Beachcomber. Now, Vivien had just gotten back from Ceylon and a few weeks of shooting *Elephant Walk*. Unhappily, she couldn't continue and was replaced by Elizabeth Taylor. As I entered the restaurant that night, Charlie greeted me and told me to pay no attention to the way Vivien was eating. There she sat, this beautiful, vulnerable, fragile woman, scooping up the food with her fingers. She, who was always most proper, did everything but lick the bowl, saying, "This is the way they eat in Ceylon." That was my first exposure to her illness. It seems that twenty years earlier, she had had a breakdown. For some reason no one could fathom, it had started up again. Vivien stayed in California for a while, had a complete mental collapse. Larry, who was in the midst of rehearsals in London, was called to bring her home. It was a traumatic time. Vivien was heart-breaking.

I next saw her in their country house in England, after she had recovered. She was quiet, still fragile, and more beautiful than ever. I cannot conceive of the torment she and Larry had undergone, but care and pain were in the air. Scrabble was the new hit game in the U.S.A., so I brought a set to Vivien; she loved games. We all played. It was a rather intimate and very special couple of days. I was so thrilled to see her—cured, I thought, but alas, the demons would not leave her alone. And they descended on Larry as well, until finally, after several difficult years, he felt his work was in jeopardy, not to mention his life. He invited me to lunch with him at the Ivy in London. That was my year in London, 1959. I was filming there at the time. He was on his way to Hollywood to make *Spartacus*. He explained to me (by then I had known he was trying to make a break) that life had become unbearable; he couldn't think, he couldn't sleep, he had much work to do and couldn't focus on it. He was going away, and he would not, could not, come back to Vivien. But he was nevertheless very concerned about her: he knew his going would add to her difficulties, and he asked me as her friend to stay close to her, to see that she was all right. He wanted least of all for her to feel abandoned by her friends. It was a painful decision for him to make, but it finally had become a question of his survival. Of course, I would not abandon her. I loved her as I did him.

Larry wrote letters from L.A. inquiring after Vivien: how was she, was I seeing her, please write. Naturally, I did. I only write about all this to demonstrate what a caring man he was—it was twenty years of his life, after all, heaven and hell. And what hell he was going through then! Though he knew he could not stay with Vivien, he also could not turn his back on her.

I was flattered to be one of the friends Larry had turned to, and all during that period I felt very close to him. A year or so later, when he fell in love with Joan Plowright, the glow that emanated from him was blinding. He dropped twenty years. To see him go from the pain of his break with Vivien to the joy of a new beginning with Joan was intoxicating. He could have a life, he had something to look forward to. There was a hiatus of several years when I did not see much of them. They were starting their family and had moved to Brighton, and my life was mostly in the States. My friendship with Vivien continued; we always spent time together in New York. She was adorable and loving, but always with an underlying sadness, never quite the same.

Gradually I got to know Joan and admire her, until now I consider myself a friend. She's a terrific woman, a terrific actress, open, down to earth, smart, and fun. She gave Larry a complete life, one he never had and never could have had with Vivien, and he totally adored her.

I attended Larry's opening performance in *Coriolanus* in Stratford-on-Avon in 1959. He had gone into training roughly six months before, and the result was remarkable. Here was a man over fifty years of age, performing the feats of a man half that. At one point in the play he stood on a part of the set that looked clifflike, twenty-five feet above the stage. His body was perfectly toned, beautiful, young, his special magic. At the end of the scene he suddenly fell, headfirst, over the parapet and hung there. The entire audience gasped as one. What a moment! There was nothing too difficult, too danger-ous, for him to try onstage. His stamina was greater than that of any other actor I have ever seen. His physicality, his beauty, all for the stage. In life he was Larry: no braggadocio, complicated, fairly quiet, sometimes wicked, often funny. Always there was an area unrevealed. That area, I suspect, was reserved for thinking about, planning, work.

He did not exude sex appeal, at least not to me, but he was playful and he loved to laugh. Privately, he was not the imposing figure of grandeur that he was in the theater. I think he fell into funny voices and stories in a room because he was a somewhat shy and serious man. It's a funny thing about sex appeal. When I see Larry now in movies like *Wuthering Heights, Rebecca, Pride and Prejudice,* and others, he exudes sex, passion, romance. Knowing him, I never saw it. I saw other things. He clearly saved that other side for work. (I have had the same reaction to Spencer Tracy, whom I felt closer to than I did to Larry. I suppose I knew him better. I look at Spence now in any of his movies—early, middle, or late in his career—and did he ever have sex appeal. Wow! Because of friendship, I had never even noticed. A major oversight!) I was never able to casually accept the fact that I knew Larry and that he actually sat through a performance of mine. What I did was so small compared to what he did.

Out of that shyness of his, that preoccupation, came the unexpected. That was the thrill of him. Onstage, he was freed of whatever inhibitions were lurking in him. You could never predict a performance. I would go backstage, head shaking in wonder at the miracle of his performance, and he would say, "Oh, my dearest, darlingest Betty, it is so lovely to see you. It is so sweet of you to come." And all accompanied by hugs and kisses. A glass of champagne was always offered, warm and welcoming, yet the gauze, the filter, that kept him from totally revealing himself would descend from time to time, so that you could still see him but not so clearly. Larry bore life scars, just as the rest of us do. He was human, after all. I could only guess at the tears, the crosscurrents that permeated his mind and heart throughout his life. I was witness to some. A dark side existed, and fortunately for him and for us, he had the stage and the screen to use as at least a partial catharsis.

The great thing that developed between Larry and me was that whenever and wherever we met, we had a history of so many years together that we could sit alone and talk about everything. In a friendship with a man like Laurence Olivier, there is so much to draw upon. We had shared years, and though I couldn't hope to breathe his rarefied air professionally, we did share a profession. He never behaved in a superior fashion with me, he talked about his work often, about the National Theatre, always candidly, the good and the not so good.

Maggie Smith, Joan Plowright, Laurence Olivier, me. A dame, a lady, a lord, and titleless me—happy to be there on the occasion of yet another Olivier honor in New York, 1980.

And he welcomed me to the London stage as an equal. He came to see me on the stage, always insisting that the management not place him where I might see him, knowing how I hated knowing when friends were out front, making sure no one told me when he'd be there. Then of course he'd come backstage, full of enthusiasm and affection. He didn't have to come—I might have wished that he would, but I didn't expect him to. Yet he did. When I was in *Sweet Bird of Youth*, he had been busy and he had been ill, but by God, he showed up on my last night. That was friendship at its best.

Larry had been out of *Dance of Death* in London for serious cancer surgery, and I happened to be in London and in the audience on his first night back. If ever there was a question of his greatness as an actor, it was dispelled that night. His performance was not of this world, it was awe-inspiring, breathtaking. Where did it come from? How did he do it? There are no answers to those questions. And how deep did he have to dig, how great a physical sacrifice was it to find the strength to perform that night? There is no answer to that one either. He didn't talk of his illness. He was very, very brave.

I remember when he was in the hospital for months with a terrifying nerve disease. I was in London then, but he was too ill to see anyone. When he was out and recovering some months later in his beloved country house, I was again in London and telephoned to see how he was coming along. He insisted on coming up to London to have tea with me in my room at the Connaught. The disease had drained him; he had to wear cotton gloves to cover his bruised hands. He couldn't dial a telephone, the pain was so great. None of it was complaint, just straightforward information. But he came through, he regained his strength, though I don't think he ever got back to what he was before he was stricken. Yet he refused to give in. He went for what kept him going—kept him alive. The theater and being a participant.

I think there is a thread that runs through each friendship and keeps it going, no words necessary. Each knows what the other knows about him, through good times and bad. When Larry looked at me, there was so much recognition in his eyes, so much affection for all the years. I will always be grateful for that.

Only now there's no Larry—there's just what I remember. So many things happen when I lose a friend. I have so many different feelings, sometimes surprising ones. I have found myself going to the phone or thinking of going to the phone, to call Mildred. Is that wishing? Desperate missing? I still do it with my mother. But there is no number to call. There is no one who will answer.

When the special friends are gone, memory is all that brings them back. Back to remind me of each emotional high I had—whether it was the discovery of Henry Moore with Mildred, Larry in *Dance of Death* and the sharing of theater, or my mother's wedding day to Lee or mine to Bogie. As I cannot believe how many friends I have had—how different they have been—so I cannot believe that so many of them are no longer here.

Memory is a precious commodity, not to be tampered with, not to be rejected. We have to be glad of its existence, for it keeps alive those special people—the moments, the places, the feelings. So, Memory, I drink to a long life—for both of us.

Life enhancer Steve Smith, a man I will never forget, a man who gave me laughter, affection, intelligence, surprises, interest, unqualified friendship—who was unlike anyone I have ever known. Someone I looked forward to—who lifted my spirits, who died too young, whose loss forever pains me and who I think of all the time. What a void he has left! How I miss him.

It was one of the best in Beverly Hills, if not the best. It was where talent and intellect from all over the world met—those who lived there and those passing through. The walls reverberated with the best show music ever written, the voices of the people who wrote it, had written it, would write it. It was where I met Vernon Duke, Solly Zuckerman, Harold Arlen,

Oscar Levant, Sidney Bernstein, Vincente Minnelli, Arthur Kober, Judy Garland, Betty Comden and Adolph Green, on and on! All who became a part of my life.

It was the home of Lee and Ira Gershwin, and what a home! You'd walk in the front door to a sea of faces—known and un; the decor was obscured by the people. Tables covered with silver trays spilling over with everything imaginable from Nate 'n' Al's deli in Beverly Hills. Modigliani unmistakable on the wall over the fireplace. Paintings by Ira of George at the piano—plus a self-portrait, a landscape.

Bogie had introduced me to the Gershwins (he'd grown up next door to Lee). He wouldn't sing along, but he did love the music, the atmosphere it created. And the great cross-section of literati and wits, from east, west, and across the seas, that filtered through and wandered in and out of that house. It was the Twenties, the Thirties —he had lived them and had had a marvelous time.

I must tell you a bit about Ira—a small, rather round man, bespectacled, fairly quiet, and of incredible sweetness. And a way of singing that brought his love of his brother and the fruits of their collaboration vibrantly alive. He allowed us to be part of that personal time. If he was not at the piano, singing Gershwin lyrics—his—to George's music, or to Harold Arlen's (Harold accompanying), he could be found in a room three steps off the living room, playing pool with Arthur Freed, Richard Brooks, and others. Bogie joined the group from time to time, as did Harry Kurnitz. Lee Gershwin made everyone feel that her home was theirs. Always welcoming, always smiling.

The house was alive. It was a breathing, vibrating, creative house, unique. Vincente Minnelli gave daughter Liza her eighth-birthday party there—gifts to the ceiling. Bogie and I brought Steve, aged four. We had a meeting there of the Committee for the First Amendment before we went to Washington. Harold played and Ira sang the score they had written for A *Star Is Born* before anyone else had heard it. The entire *Porgy and Bess* company, with William

Warfield and Clamma Dale, came to a fabulous party there, after their last performance, celebrating that Gershwin work. The best of times!

You'd hear music. Someone at the piano. It might be Harold Arlen, it might be Oscar Levant. And it was where, in the early Fifties, I met Leonard Bernstein.

He was dazzling, electric. The mutual attraction was instant. We were both happily married, but the attraction was there anyway. He sat at the piano, playing Gershwin. We all gathered round and sang along. I have always been hooked on show tunes played on a piano in a living room.

Lenny, as I was instantly instructed to call him, exuded energy. It was impossible not to feel it, not to be affected by it. Bogie not only recognized the talent, the uniqueness of the man, but he knew that if there was a piano in a room and someone to play it, I was a goner and doomed to stay up until the wee small hours. He also knew that I was a romantic, a chameleon, and deeply impressionable. In fact, he knew everything about me, better than I did myself. But being a man of great instinct and wisdom, attraction or no attraction, he did not feel threatened. And of course, as usual, he was right. Though if Lenny and I had been on the loose, God knows what madness might have taken over. Had I been left to my own whims and fantasies during those young years, I dread to think of the mistakes I would have made. Though I have to say that being joined to Bogie enabled me to be much braver than I ever would have been on my own.

On one trip, Lenny was overseeing the playing of his music at the Hollywood Bowl. At his invitation, I went to watch a rehearsal —Bogie had gone on a major boat race around the Channel Islands —and I vividly remember him sitting alone in a box in the empty Bowl as Johnny Green conducted the Los Angeles Philharmonic. (Lenny would conduct his own "Serenade.") I sat off to one side watching him. Black cape tossed over his shoulders, he listened intently, very seriously, a study in absorption, all outside influences shut

This photo was given to me by Lenny—dedicated to me and treasured by me.

out: a lone figure with his lion's head, sitting in the middle of this vast outdoor concert hall.

Another time he was guest pianist at the same Bowl, playing *Rhapsody in Blue*. My first view of him as a professional pianist: not only playing brilliantly but with his theatricality, which was so much a part of him, bringing extra excitement to the performance. Lenny was a dashing, romantic figure, exuberant, bursting with enthusiasm about everything, everyone; brilliant, dedicated, and ever mysterious. Mysterious as all who have that special gift are. There was an immediacy to him. Everything was focused on now, now was what it was all about, the peak of life was now. He was contagious, and he had that extra something—a calling: he was a star. There was music to be composed, pianos to be played, symphonies to conduct, the young to teach. It was often said of Lenny that had he followed any one of his talents—as composer, conductor, teacher, or concert pianist—he would have achieved greatness. As it was, at that period in his life he was bursting with all four, so there was no doubt that he would go where he had to go and do what he had to do. He often—more than likely always—took his music with him.

On one trip to Los Angeles, he had come to our house to swim or to play tennis and had brought with him his score for *Trouble in Tahiti*. It was about to be performed in Germany, and as it was an opera, it had to be translated and amended. I'd never before seen anything like what he was doing. It was stunning, that complete focus. Sitting in our library, he was transported to another country, another language. It was on that day that Bogie said of Lenny: "He's not like us. You could never keep up with him. He's got places to go and things to do. He's a genius." The fascinating lesson in all this was the realization that when he entered that part of his life, he was alone. No one could share it, or could understand it. When he was with me his attention was total, but I always felt that when he left, he did not take me with him. We both knew we would always be friends, always part of each other's lives. We talked about everything together, easily, openly. He was constantly working on something. He told me he spent hours in his studio, alone; how much he loved it and how hard it was at times. The first piece I'd ever seen him conduct, unforgettably, was Brahms's Second Symphony—again at the Bowl—which led me to his Fourth and, conducted by Lenny, to his violin concerto. From then on I could never think of Brahms without Bernstein.

As the years wore on, our friendship shifted gears. After my move to New York, I found myself meeting him and his wife, Felicia, at mutual friends' and being invited to their apartment. Gradually I became part of the nucleus of close friends who shared evenings with them. I never figured out how that happened, but invitations were extended by Felicia, who knew instinctively that Lenny and I had special feelings for each other. She was an unusual woman—cultured, talented, beautiful, smart, and funny. A perfect wife for Lenny. Everyone adored her, me included.

They both were dedicated to righting wrongs, fighting social injustice, discrimination of any kind. Lenny cared about so many things: how he had the time to even think about it all I don't know, plus being a devout family man and a deeply religious man. His ego was enormous—so large that one was kind of swept along with it.

He could be infuriating. There were times when I would happily have strangled him. But he was never dull. Entering the Bernstein home, you had to be prepared: his personality was so overpowering that you sometimes had to fight to keep your own. He was sure of his opinions, sure he was right. Outspoken—more than once in our relationship he said things that were hurtful, not meaning to, just talk off the top of his head. I knew how fond of me he was, but there was something in him that couldn't help knocking you at times, making him seem insensitive. Once I called him on a remark of his, and he was shocked to think he had hurt me. "I would never hurt you. You know that. I love you." That was Lenny.

We ended up living in the same building, two floors apart. When Lenny and Felicia bought their New York apartment, I was living in England. I offered them my place while they were renovating theirs, and they lived there for several months. So from 1974 to the end of their lives, we kind of shared the same space and I perhaps saw more of them than I might have otherwise.

When Felicia became ill with cancer, she made Lenny promise to try to stop smoking. So he and I and Patrick O'Neal met once a week with the founder of SmokEnders to give up the deadly addiction. It worked for me for eight and a half months, and enabled me to stop completely after seven more attempts, seven years ago. Patrick went through much the same off-and-on routine that I did. Lenny, however, was hopeless. He tried—desperately—and just couldn't make it. He'd sneak one in the bathroom, go out on an errand, anyplace, so Felicia wouldn't see. But he had to have that one cigarette when he had to have it. Felicia, of course, finally did know he hadn't beaten the habit, but he did not smoke in her presence. Nor did I—nor did Patrick.

Oh, that was a sad year, the agony of Felicia's illness—the toll it took on her body, his head, and their children. She, the core of

Me with Lenny at Wolf Trap—celebrating his sixtieth, 1978.

his family, the one who held it together—going. And finally gone. He would sometimes ask if Bogie's symptoms or reactions had been the same as Felicia's. At least he knew he had a friend whose loss had been the equal of his and who could commiserate with him. Far from the best bond in the world, but a bond nonetheless. An unexpected one.

Lenny tried and succeeded in setting aside time for composing. His conducting life was planned two years ahead, sometimes more. The months set aside were precious to him: days concentrating on creating his music, occasionally in collaboration with a librettist, but often alone. And his frustration when he couldn't write fast enough or enough, period, depressed him greatly.

I thought Lenny would go on forever. It never occurred to me that it could be otherwise. He had had emphysema for years. He seemed constantly under pressure, with perpetual demands on his time. If not traveling all over the world to conduct, he was in his special composing mode—very private. He seemed continually to be celebrated for various reasons: a new production of *Candide*, or a concert version of *West Side Story* for television, or musical anniversaries in London or Israel, or conducting the first free concert at the fallen Berlin Wall, or an amazing, unforgettable night in Central Park. Then came his seventieth birthday. In every country, every city he visited, there was a celebration. The last one, and the most meaningful to him, was at Tanglewood in Massachusetts, where he himself had started and where he had taught young musicians all his musical life.

I couldn't believe it. Steve Sondheim was at the other end of the phone: "I am writing special lyrics to the music of *Jenny* from *Lady in the Dark* for Lenny's seventieth. Will you do it?" I was flattered, surprised, thrilled—and with Steve Sondheim, as always impressed. "For Lenny," said I, "of course. I'll die—but of course." And I thought, Not only to be part of the event but to sing—God help me. At last I would have the opportunity to work with Stephen Sondheim. Not exactly a show, but something. Was I nervous? I'll say. Both singing for Steve and singing to Lenny terrified me, and on the big night I was the last one scheduled to perform.

Adrenaline does work, does keep you going, on such a night: I so wanted to be good for Lenny, for Steve, and for me. Four hours of pacing backstage with fluttering heart and shaking hands. And an enormous amount of deep breathing. On cue, I walked onto that stage, faced the audience of well over a thousand people. Lenny's box was spotlighted, so all could direct their attention to him. Steve sitting down front, accompanist Paul Ford on stage with me, microphone and stool (a must for possible buckling of knees). I got through it! What a feeling! It was the final oversize celebration of Lenny's seventy years, and though it was exhausting for him—the end of a year of such happenings worldwide—it was a great night, full of love. Friends and colleagues from all over the world flew in for the occasion and worked on their contributions as they would for a concert, an opera, a show. Everyone wanted it to be the best for Lenny. Those moments of frustration and annoyance with him were far outweighed by real affection, and this was a chance to perhaps give something back.

Then suddenly—though in fact it was not so sudden—he became ill, visibly ill. There was exhaustion, emphysema, and more exhaustion. He had to cancel a concert—a trip to Japan, where another award was to be bestowed on him—and then the announcement. His daughter Jamie and son Alexander called to tell me of it, not wanting me to read it in the paper. He was retiring from conducting. The travel, the life—all of it was too much for him. A shock—not Lenny! But finally even he had to face the limits of his body.

I had seen him a couple of times. He had been resting in his country house. I had been away working and returned a day before my birthday. Lenny and I shared zodiac signs. There was, as always, a message from him. This time a note: "Ah—love—what have we Virgos done to deserve this. But as long as there is love—and there is — x x x—Lenny."

I went to visit him, two floors down, before leaving for England. He was sitting in a chair, watching the news. We shared a drink, some words of affection—mine: that if he'd listen he'd be well again soon; his: "I'm stunned, it's all happened so fast." He looked at me—studying me—said, "You're so beautiful, I forgot how beautiful you are." Something he might have said when we'd just met. I instantly changed the subject, as usual being unable to deal with that kind of compliment. I kissed him goodbye and left, not thinking for a moment that I'd never see him again.

A few days after my arrival in London, I saw his face on the television screen in my hotel room. It happened so fast. I still see him so clearly—on the podium, in his apartment with the three children he cherished above all, the grandchildren and friends, always friends. He graced my life.

I t was a new world to me. Picture this: eighteen years old, entering a house that looked like a hotel to these New York apartment eyes. Actually, it was a beautiful ranch, Howard and Slim Hawks style. In Slim's walk-in closet, the size of your average bedroom, I saw sweaters folded neatly on open shelves, a wall of handbags hanging on hooks, shoes side by side by endless side, and racks of clothes of all shapes and colors—all the best, Slim style.

My friendship with Jean Howard, Charlie Feldman's wife, and Slim Hawks began when I was under contract to Charlie. It's hard to develop a friendship with your employer or his wife, so I would say Slim and I got along from the start, recognizing immediately that we'd have hit it off under any circumstances.

Slim had had a good life, an interesting one, and she'd been having health problems off and on for ten or fifteen years. They'd gotten worse during the last four or five. I would call her when I was at home of an evening, and we'd catch up on everything with a phone conversation that could last an hour. Her health truly started to fail in November 1989. There was a memorial service for Diana Vreeland at the Metropolitan Museum of Art and at the end of it, as I was walking

Slim with Howard Hawks on the lawn of their beautiful Bel Air farm, 1944.

out, I saw Slim, in a wheelchair. It was a shocking sight. I immediately went over to give her a hug and a kiss. Slim said, "This is what I hate —I hate this." Not the hug and the kiss: the wheelchair. You see, she was always a vital, energetic mover, not one to be confined. Now she had lost her choice. She said, "Call me." I did the next day, and we made a date to have dinner and go to a screening of *Driving Miss Daisy.*

At last we were to have a full long evening together. A catch-up evening. I was so looking forward to it. Why hadn't I called before? The morning of our date, she called to tell me she'd had a funny heart flutter and the doctor had told her she was to stay in bed. I had to go to St. Louis for a lecture the next day and called her the second I returned, only to learn that she'd had a heart attack and was in the hospital. In intensive care with a telephone. In this particular hospital, her branch of intensive care meant a shared room—one other occupant. And being hooked up to the dreaded machines that recorded every flutter of her stuttering heart. Only Slim would have a telephone in intensive care. She had called and left a lengthy message on my answering machine. And a phone number. My clue that she was in real trouble, aside from the obvious one, was that she repeated the same story to me several times.

I called her. She sounded somewhat weak, short of breath, but wanted to see me, told me a good time to come, when it might be quieter, not too many distractions. When I arrived, there was no one else there, and she was asleep.

Hospitals have a disquieting effect on most people. To me, they represent a multitude of visions: of my mother; and of Bogie; and of my son Steve, who had a hernia operation at age two and a half; and of my daughter, Leslie, who had a bad attack of asthma after the death of her father, when she was five. The happy hospital times, the births of my three children, are overpowered by the sad and terror-filled times, the tiptoeing down painted corridors and the whispering.

I had seen Slim when she took to her bed after her mother died and when Leland Hayward left her, but I had never seen her in bed with disks attached to her body. I stood there and watched her. At last she opened her eyes. After my signature hug and kiss, she proceeded to give me the lowdown on her diagnosis. She was overflowing with medical talk: doctors, her lack of health, how she felt about staying alive in the shape she was in. She was not crazy about the idea. I, as I had before with her, said, "Of course you must do anything that will improve the situation, and you'd better hang around a lot longer —there are quite a few of us who love you." The thing about a friendship like ours—what made it so special—was that it didn't matter a damn that our lives were different, that we didn't see each other regularly or even talk to each other regularly; the bond was so strong, the affection so deep, our mutual fragility so obvious to us, that we didn't need all that other stuff. She was whisked away, under protest, to Michigan (if it was Michigan) and returned a few days later. When I called, she said she didn't think any magic had been performed and wasn't convinced it had been worth the trip.

On Friday morning, around nine a.m. the phone rang. It

was Jerry Robbins, calling to tell me she had gone. An eerie thing happens to me before someone I am very close to dies. I seem to know. It manifests itself in nonstop sobbing the day and night before, as it did with my mother and Bogie, or in not being able to think about much else and wanting to talk to the person, as it did with Slim; it's a kind of ESP, though I don't really attribute it to that. Anyway, it's something inexplicable. And then I thought of all the years known and all the times shared and the sight of her in the hospital when I left her laughing hysterically at an outrageous story I had stolen from David Niven—those ghastly disks jiggling up and down as her body shook with laughter—and I felt so good that I'd been able to give her that minute of pleasure. Slim's death was another ending, and it leaves a one-sided friendship, which in turn leaves yet another unfillable hole in my very punctured spirit.

Slim's was a different kind of friendship and love, but it was both, nevertheless. I was an eighteen-year-old virgin child. She introduced me to adult life, to a professional life, and to what was to be the best part of my emotional life.

The ties that bound us were those, plus a built-in unexplainable female bond of understanding. She was a beauty with an original mind, and she responded to my mind. I was shaped by her husband to be the celluloid Slim, so we were, of course, inextricably bound. She was irresistible because, among other things, she responded to my humor. And she laughed out loud and completely. And I was oh so glad of that, because I felt she had an enormously sad center. I never mentioned it to her, but I felt it. And though we liked each other and became instant friends, it couldn't be an equal friendship, because she did discover me and her husband made me a star and owned me contractually. He was my boss, and she was the boss's wife. Even so, she was on my side, as she was when I dissolved in tears after Howard Hawks told me he would sell my contract to Monogram—a studio known for B pictures—if I didn't stop behaving like a fool over Bogart. She tried to make him see how hard it was for me, but she didn't succeed. After all, he was losing his star creation; Svengali was being out-Svengalied by an actor. And she did have to live with him. Then, by the time I married Bogie and Howard sold my contract (to Warner's), Slim and I had stopped seeing each other.

When Bogie wanted to buy me a present, his first, she had gone with him to choose it. It was a gold identification bracelet with my name on the outside and "The Whistler" engraved on the inside. So as long as the bracelet and I are together—and we still are—Slim will be part of my life.

It wasn't until she was married to Leland Hayward and they started coming to California for Leland's movies that our friendship developed in a real and grown-up way. We had many mutual friends and frequented each other's houses. During the years of Bogie's final illness, the Haywards rented a house just across the street from ours, so I was able to visit with Slim easily and fairly often. And after Bogie's death, our friendship grew stronger. She was so good for me, so smart. I was able to talk to her—not really deep confidences, not that I had that many. But at a time when I needed to talk, she listened and helped with her listening.

When I was really desperate, a year after Bogie's death, when I had to get out of California—when she told me I had to get out—she saved my sanity and my life by coming to Spain with me, a trip that unknowingly started the disintegration of her life.

On that Spanish trip I went wild—well, wild for me. It was my first exposure to the seductiveness of flamenco and anisette. I was introduced to her old friends—my new ones—Aline and Luis Quintanilla, who took us to a great flamenco club in Madrid with some on-the-loose Spanish men. I wore a great black crepe Norman Norell dress with bare shoulders, flat, inch-wide straps, strands of crepe all around from rib to knee, which swung with every step. After the floor show and several glasses of anisette (very strong stuff), I found myself twirling around, streamers flying, hands clapping, doing my own version of flamenco. Slim's laughing face spurred me on.

We shared a suite in the Castellana Hilton. Its round living room with balcony had a bedroom and bath on either side. We had gone out with some Spaniards, one of whom had taken a fancy to me. He was handsome and young, though not too, perfectly nice and Spanish and new. I was in a fragile emotional state, desperately trying to find a place for myself and someone who cared about me. Slim wanted to go to bed after dinner. My date wanted to take me for a drink. So we went for a drink. Then he insisted on coming up the elevator with me, and at my door insisted on coming inside for an additional drink. And in he came. Of course, he had ideas other than the drink. Slim was sitting up in bed, reading, with her door slightly ajar. He kissed me, and after a little friendly feel I thought it was time for him to go. He would have none of it, and before I knew what was happening I was on the run, with him in hot pursuit. In a round room, that was dizzy-making. As I passed Slim's door I skidded to a stop, pushed it open, and said to her astonished face, "What do I do now?" At each of my pit stops at her door, she would look up and dissolve in hysterical laughter. Finally I'd had enough—he wouldn't give up. I called out to my friend, "How do I get rid of this guy?" Desperate now, not to mention out of breath. Whereupon she replied, in her Slim fashion, "Do it!" So I did. And I still don't believe that I did.

I don't think I could have done anything like that with anyone else.

After that we went to Paris, where Leland was to meet us and where Slim would introduce me to Pamela Churchill, the woman who was to be a factor in the demise of her marriage to Leland. And it was Slim who came with me to Spain much later when I was making a movie there, and took me down to Málaga to meet Ernest Hemingway. His novel *To Have and Have Not* was the basis for my first movie.

I was with her through her traumatic split with Leland. We

Reinaldo Herrera—following the bulls the summer of 1959, the year
of the *mano a mano* between Dominguin and Ordonès.

At the airport with Slim before leaving Málaga, having a drink with Papa Hemingway, 1959.

spent that summer of 1958 in Biarritz with our children, trying to recover our centers, be mothers, feel better, and hide our terrible lack of confidence from the outside world. We were very alike then. We shared a great deal of pain, and we understood what that meant. Yet we still managed to laugh a lot. So despite Slim's pure Aryan heritage —she'd been well-born, was used to servants and houses and greenery —and my pure Jewish heritage (I was well-born but not in the financial sense and was used to doing-it-yourself and apartments and cement), we were very similar. We identified with each other: the "Slim" Connection. I think we behaved with each other as we never did or could have or would have with anyone else.

Still, I have never been able to solve the dichotomy of her. She was too intelligent to spend her time surrounded by, or submerged in, superficiality, though she did spend a great deal of time doing not much of anything. Then again, those are my work judgments. I don't understand open-ended leisure. When she moved to England and became Lady Keith to her husband's Sir, she ran a perfectly appointed household, as she always had in California and New York. She involved herself in charities—the Tate, a hospital, and like activities— with weekends at her husband's beautiful estate. There was the pheasant season, then quail, then ducks; she shopped in the most expensive and tasteful antique shops. She led a highfalutin privileged life, come to think of it. At the same time, she loved and appreciated talent and could and always did pick up where she left off with old chums. She didn't belong to England; she wasn't happy there. I don't think she ever found her place after Leland. With that great brain and those great looks, she could have done so much more. I say that not in judgment but because even at her happiest she continued to be restless, not quite satisfied. Unfulfilled.

I found the last part of her life sad. Though she didn't really complain. She was a self-described "nest maker." "That's what I do," she would say. "You're an actress—that's *your* work. Mine is making nests." Only it was sad, to me at least, because after Leland there was really no one worthy to make a nest for. Such a shame—she was so good at it.

At her memorial I was the very first to speak and nervously told the story of what we'd referred to as the Spanish incident, that memorable night in the Castellana. I wasn't at all sure how it would be received by those present, but it revealed a side of Slim that most folks were not privy to. I knew she would have loved it; her beautiful daughter, Kitty, did, and to my immense relief, friends and family present laughed. It is a great sound to hear on such a very sad occasion. A Slim sound.

What I see now when I think of her is the very first time I saw her, walking into her living room, where Howard Hawks and I were sitting: a tall young golden girl of incredible good looks—very, very Slim—on her way to lunch, putting on her short white gloves, smiling, friendly, no strain, and healthy. An outdoor California girl. She was sunshine.

In my autobiography, *By Myself,* I wrote in some detail about my introduction to, experiences with, and memories of John Huston. Of his enduring and close relationship with Bogie. All of which took place between 1945 and 1974.

It was clear to me then that he was a man of most special talents, with a personality belonging only to himself. He took me to uncharted waters, and I always knew he would leave an indelible mark on my life. Through the years, thoughts of him have often risen to the surface, and, I suspect, they will remain with me to the end of my days. I never did find out what drove him, what made him tick, but finally I have decided that's not important. Between 1945 and his death in 1987, I saw enough sides of the man to learn of his fleeting interest in almost anything, his impatience with life, and his wit and majesty in getting through it.

What follows now is his last years—what I was fortunate enough to witness, be a part of—and what they left me.

. . .

John Huston and his son Danny had come to see me to talk about appearing in a movie, *Mr. North*, which John had written and planned to star in, with Danny directing. Anything to do with John Huston and work was to me much the same as with Robert Altman today—an automatic go, absolutely, just tell me when.

It was to be shot in Newport, Rhode Island, an old-money social community I had never and would never have entered save for John and *Mr. North*.

He had been fighting emphysema for years, had been in and out of wheelchairs, with oxygen his constant companion. But he wouldn't give in. His behavior was spectacular. He was always a larger-than-life man, and this experience added yet another dimension to this complex, multi-sided man.

Unhappily, the day before we started shooting, his illness took over and he was unable to work. He lasted through the shooting and spent the last weeks of his life in a hospital and the last days in his rented house, with all his children around him. Before all this disaster, he'd presided over a small dinner with Anjelica, Danny, myself, and some other members of the cast, during which we reminisced about Africa and days gone by. They were fun and laughing stories, so it was a happy evening.

And I thought then and after, and reflect now, on what a major part John played in my life: through all my married years with Bogie; through Bogie's illness and the eulogy he delivered at Bogie's memorial; through providing two of our greatest out-of-the-country adventures, in Mexico and Africa, and taking part in some of our funniest, most outrageous times in various world capitals; as one of the leaders of our trip to Washington during the horrible Hollywood investigation years. He never stopped being fascinating, brilliant, funny, mad, and infuriating.

I have never met and I'm sure there has never been anyone remotely like him. He gave me an awareness of writers I had never heard of, such as B. Traven, Stephen Crane, W. R. Burnett. He had the gift of words and ideas; he was always searching, and I'm not sure he was ever happy. Generally, I don't think he liked women—when he was humiliating a wife, it was deeply unnerving—but he was able to like me because I was Bogie's wife.

All he did, he did in his own Huston way. He loved his father, Walter; he loved Bogie; he loved Anjelica, Danny, Tony, and Allegra; and that was about it I would say. And all through his devastating, painful illness, he, like Bogie, never complained. He left an unfillable space in work and life. He contributed knowledge, adventure, and excitement that was original and unique to him and that cannot be duplicated.

His relationship with Bogie began long before I came on the scene. Both of them were at Warner's—John a writer, Bogie an actor—until *The Maltese Falcon* and Bogie's willingness to take a chance on this writer's first directorial effort. They were not personally alike, really: Bogie wanting a more stable life, a saner one; John more driven, being quite incapable of staying in any one place too long. They made each other laugh. They challenged each other's work—each reaching higher because of the other—and finally they respected each other.

They both were professionals, perfectionists, and they both were devils—drank well together, enjoyed the working of each other's minds, disagreed, fought mildly—and very occasionally they were slightly cuckoo, both of them always fun to be around, though unpredictable and prankish. Like John bringing home a monkey as a pet, playing touch football at his house at three in the morning, tweaking and twisting Bogie's nose one drunken evening in Africa—the result of one of those wild disagreements. But they loved each other.

This was no ordinary friendship. They were together socially a great deal, but in actual fact, spent such an enormous amount of time together because in addition they worked together so often and so well. Their personalities each had an edge, so in that way they were very alike. That was part of the mutual attraction. Bogie may not have gone along with all of John's life choices, but he did understand his personal problems. And he empathized with them. And John was able to talk to Bogie, whom he knew he could trust and who he knew would be honest with him. Not only did they enjoy each other, but each of them recognized the uniqueness of the other—how they stood out and rose above the ordinariness of so many around them. When John would cast a picture, Bogie was almost always the first choice; and when Bogie was asked by John to join him in moviemaking, there was no question about Bogie's saying yes. He always felt that as high as you might go with another director, with John you could always go

1948 or 1949 at John Huston's house in Tarzana with the famous monkey—not everybody's favorite thing, but loving Bogie trying to get him drunk. We all—Joyce Buck and Evelyn Keyes included—approved.

higher. At the same time, John's attention span was fairly short and his boredom level easily reached. Bogie, ever aware of this failing, always kept a weather eye and pulled him back into the proper finishing of the movie. John was dazzling. He drew people to him like a magnet. You had to be careful not to be too drawn—at least not to the exclusion of everything else, for John was a love-'em-and-leave-'em kind of guy. He would see you, and you would be convinced you were the one person in the world he wanted to see. The hugs, the enthusiasm, the Hello, honeys! But when you left or he did, you had to know you were forgotten: you were only in *that* moment of John's life. But he did mean it—at the time. I still always felt lucky to have had that moment. After all, John was not like anyone else.

Having been with him in Mexico for two months and in Africa and London for four or more, I was able to observe him in his directing mode quite often. With Bogie he had unspoken communication. I never knew what the shorthand was specifically, but I knew that when they talked about a scene they figured it out, and then in the shooting of that same scene, if the result was not quite what John wanted, eye contact and a word or two seemed to be enough. That kind of connection is so rare as to be almost nonexistent. Is it any wonder they worked together every chance they could? The locations were always difficult, not easily accessible—part of the attraction for John. Bogie beefed, but he would always go; partly, I think, because he was incredulous and because he wanted to see for himself how far John would go.

On *The Treasure of the Sierra Madre*, John was very much the same with his father, Walter, except that it was the first time they had worked together and the joy and personal pride they had in each other was palpable. Walter impressed with John's ability, and John thrilled to be giving Walter the role of a lifetime. As John was a man who did not openly or, I daresay, easily deal with his emotions, watching him soften, open up a little more with Walter, becoming somewhat vulnerable, therefore more human, more connected, made the hours spent with him there all the more moving.

I experienced his creative gifts firsthand in *Key Largo*. He was articulate with actors: he knew what he wanted and told you. But he told you privately. An arm around your shoulder, a walk away from the set to explain. Never to embarrass; never to make you feel uncomfortable. It is difficult to isolate specifics in John the director. Friend or not, he was the figure of authority on the set. He had a gift for listening to anyone working on the picture. Working with John was an exchange of ideas—it was a cooperative effort. John instilled trust; I certainly trusted him in *Key Largo*, wanted his help and got it. As in my last scene in *Key Largo*: after a tense exchange between the Bogart and Edward G. Robinson characters, there I was with my father, Lionel Barrymore, worried that I would never see Bogart again. The phone rang, with the Bogie character telling me he was on his way back to me. It could have been a soapy moment—instead of which, it was quite real. Me telling Lionel he was returning to us; filled with emotion. I had to cross the room to Lionel, go to the window, open the shutters to let the sunlight in, signaling the start of a new day and hope. It was John's idea to open the shutters. Another visual that said more than words ever could.

He was a friend to me. Not the kind of friend I would call in the middle of the night for help—though, come to think of it, he'd probably have rushed right over. So I guess I would say he was not a day-to-day friend. His interests were elsewhere, and they were many and far-flung. He had been a boxer in his youth, had always loved horses, riding to hounds, as he did in Ireland. He was a writer, a lover of the written and spoken word. And a lover of art—paintings, sculpture. I had never heard of pre-Columbian art until John, who had an extraordinary collection of it. For no apparent reason, I hadn't expected him to live in great style. I was totally wrong. His house in Tarzana, California, which he designed and built, was in keeping with his size: large, expansive, comfortable, modern—mixed with antique furniture—different kinds of wood, a perfect background for his pre-Columbian art display. You can see in his movies how uniquely visual he was. He saw people and places in a way nobody else did.

I didn't see much of him for a few years after Bogie's death.

John backstage at *Cactus Flower* after surprising me with his appearance
and again with his approval, 1967.

He lived in Ireland; invited me numerous times. Stupidly, I never
went. He was never happy about my second marriage, though he
never said so. But I knew. He wanted me with Bogie or no one. That's
who I was to him.

Though John had talked to me a couple of times about
appearing in something he was developing, those projects unhappily
were never done. To him I was first and foremost Bogie's wife. I never
thought of John as being a true lover and enjoyer of women, except as
possible conquests. Wives should be at home with their husbands.
Wives should bear children and, almost always, or preferably, speak
only when spoken to. I think he was genuinely fond of me but that a
lot of it was because he associated me with good and happy times
when all of us were working together. On the locations, I was the
nonworking tagalong wife looking after her husband, and we had great
times together. Then during Bogie's illness and after, in John's eyes I

behaved as a wife should behave. Because of the closeness we had all shared, and because Bogie and I were such a complete pair, any man who might come into my life was looked upon as an interloper. How dare he! John was a macho man, and perhaps it was my insecurity with him that made me feel as I've described. It certainly did not hamper our relationship. In fact, it probably made it a stronger one than most women had with him. Anyway, it lasted a hell of a long time and saw us through the best: the birth of children, the rewards of work well done, and the shared laughter of friendship and the worst of life, sickness, and death.

In the most unforgettable and probably my favorite memory of John, it is early morning in Africa—he is in safari pants and jacket, brown slouch hat, brown boots, brown cigarillo in hand. In kingly fashion John is waving, smiling, and bowing to the natives who lined the route daily as we headed for the Ruiki River for the day's shooting. Pure, beautiful Huston.


Before *Mr. North* was to start shooting, John had had one or two bouts in a hospital. He lived in Mexico, had always loved Mexico: no doors, no windows, no shoes. An easy climate, easy living. I guess he might be called something of a nomad, a free spirit. With his illness and the need for periodic medical attention, Mexico was not all that practical. I later learned that he had telephoned Robert Mitchum before leaving Los Angeles for Newport, to ask if he would be willing to take over John's role in the movie in the event that John became incapable of the work. Mitchum, being a classy man, said of course. And as it turned out, on the first day of shooting John had an emphysema attack and *was* unable to work. A call was placed to Bob, and he arrived the following day. Although John improved slightly, he never was well enough to perform. So the movie was made under the worst possible conditions. A beautiful location, but endless pressure for Danny, who was constantly worried about his father while trying to concentrate on directing his first fairly major motion picture, plus making script changes. A hopelessly unfair job. And Anjelica worried, and those of us who were old friends worried. All in all, I am amazed the movie turned out as well as it did, given these obstacles.

I visited John several times in the hospital. He was an impressive figure even there, asking me how the work was going, telling me how good it was for me to visit, how good to see me. All the while, shortness of breath was a major problem. He asked me how Danny was doing, and we talked of Anjelica—what a beauty she was, how happy he was to have her there with him. How glad that his son Tony and his other daughter, Allegra, had come over from England to spend time with him. I could plainly see how hard it was for him to speak. He never referred to that. Never complained. When I suggested it was time for me to leave, that he must rest, he said, "All right, honey—thanks for coming." I kissed him goodbye, as I did the other times I visited, never thinking that this goodbye kiss would be the last.

It's interesting that the man who was a self-designated non-family man should have spent so much time talking about his children. But I shouldn't have been surprised. John was never predictable. He had always lived with great extravagance. Never being content with less than the best—in work, food, clothes, and in houses created by him. He had a grandeur about him, an Old World quality. And he traveled best alone. Necessary to feed his restless nature. Because of all his extraordinary qualities, I was always a bit anxious in his presence, wanting to please him, amuse him, and, most of all, hold his attention. I always felt I was in the presence of the Master. And I was right to feel that. He *was* the Master.

· · ·

I have spent a good deal of time trying to figure friendship out, without much luck. Why one friendship survives whether people see each other or not, why another fades for no apparent reason. Why sometimes old friends are easy to talk to about everything and then impossible to talk to about anything.

Years ago, John Huston said that what matters most in any relationship—certainly in friendship—is interest. Those special friends whom I am closest to do just that. They interest me: how they think, what they feel, how they deal with life—its gifts and its denials. They add to and complete the circle of my life and enrich me. They are what I hang on to.

# BEGINNINGS AND ENDINGS

J ust when you think you've done most of it—
children grown and well, not unscarred but
out of the nest and doing just fine dealing with their own lives, no
major parental decisions needing to be made—just when you think
that, the telephone rings.

That's what happened to me two years ago. My daughter—
beautiful, funny, independent Leslie—announced that she was going
to be married. And guess what: a new experience was in store for me.
I, the sole surviving parent, would be giving the wedding. I knew she
and Erich had been living together for more than a year, but there
had been other close calls, serious, long-term relationships. I had
wished for so long that Leslie would find someone she wanted to share
her life with—the way Steve and Sam had done—that this time I was
either too involved with my own life and work or just determined to
stop thinking along those lines for fear of another disappointment. Yet
here it was, by God, it had happened. Erich had happened: he had
proposed, she had accepted. *He*, expert yoga teacher; *she*, yoga thera-
pist; *they*, shared interests—it should make for a super union. But how

do I begin? With sons, you're a joyous guest—all you have to do is be there and enjoy. With daughters, it all depends on you: that's what I thought, but I was only partly right. Leslie had her own ideas. She and Erich would plan and decide what they wanted, and where. Whoa! All well and good, but where do I come in? This was a first for both of us. I'd never given a wedding. Leslie had never had one. We'd have to start somewhere. When you're in your twenties, it's simple (ha!)—but when you've been living on your own and waited to take this plunge until you're thirty-seven, there's no "ha" about it.

At first Leslie thought she would wait a year—"Sam and Suzy did." "But they were twenty-three, darling. You've waited thirty-seven years before making the commitment." The date would have to coincide with their having a month's free honeymoon time. She may have been thirty-seven, but she *felt* twenty-three.

Leslie has never been one to be overdemonstrative. She has been rather understated. She has a great wit—a wry wit, original—yet there is also a shyness about her. Granted, she has usually been more reserved with me; we love each other, respect each other, share the same humor, but we are different, with different goals, interests, life-styles. She has less interest in having a permanent base than I had. When I was her age, I'd had two children, lost one husband, gained another, and had another child. I love to travel but have always needed a base to return to, with my things around me, my security. Thus far she does not have that need. Partly because she hates cities—needs clean air and trees. She's a nature girl and hasn't settled on the particular place yet.

The where of the wedding would be California, where Erich's family lived and where their many friends and even Sam and Suzy (who were working there at the time) were. That meant travel for only Steve, Barbara, and me.

I knew I would have to go to California for two weeks to get things organized. I knew there'd be surprises, things neither Leslie nor I had thought of. And I prayed it would all come right, be what she wanted and what I wanted for her.

I found myself feeling hypersensitive, feeling somewhat of an outsider in a peculiar way. She was my daughter, my only daughter, and my last child to be married. I did not like what I felt. Bogie's not being there, my being the sole parent, not being able to stand side by side with the father of my children as they set off to try their hands at their own growing-up lives. How different it would have been with Bogie around. I realized how raw my emotions had become—not a case of self-pity, more a case of being clobbered all at once with all the emotions that weddings bring to the surface.

Leslie decided she wanted to be married in Sam and Suzy's backyard in the afternoon, with the reception to be held at one of our favorite restaurants. To order the invitations, we entered a charming shop on Montana Avenue, the street of dreams that leaves you wanting things you never thought you wanted before—and buying them. Dangerous.

Leslie chose the recycled paper she wanted for the announcements, then came the emotional (for me) wording. I had made up my mind to have Bogie's name on the announcement. She was *his* only daughter too, and I somehow felt that this was necessary—coming full circle, in a way. Most wedding announcements read: "Mr. and Mrs. Blank are happy to announce the marriage of their daughter —— to Blank." Leslie's obviously could not read that way. After giving it endless thought, I arrived at what seemed to me a stroke of genius (she said modestly). "Leslie Bogart, daughter of Lauren Bacall and the late Humphrey Bogart, is marrying Erich Schiffmann, etc., etc." Pause. Tension began to rear its ugly head. Leslie wanted her name next to Erich's. I said that couldn't be. I, her mother, was making the announcement. It couldn't read Leslie Bogart and Erich Schiffmann, daughter of etc.

Leslie kept drawing diagrams, trying to figure out a way to have Leslie and Erich together first, with parents ending up God knows where. By this time my stomach was so knotted it didn't feel like a stomach at all. This was it—our first head-on collision. "Do what you want, Leslie." Then she said—tossing down the pencil that had been unable to draw the desired result—"All right, whatever you want to do." I couldn't see any other way to word the announcement. The patient salesgirl, clearly having witnessed moments like this before, came to the rescue. She printed a mock-up of it so Leslie could see with her own eyes what it would look like. Tensions eased; truce declared; conversation resumed; mother and daughter friends again, guardedly aware that friction could well strike again.

For me, emotion and remembrance struck, with a vengeance. Mapleton Drive. Leslie had entered that house at five days old. Bogie was alive. We had a home, a family life, dogs, successful careers, his anyway. I was happy then. It lasted such a short time after that. I wanted magnolia leaves from that house, cut from the same trees that had produced the leaves at Bogie's memorial service. I wanted those leaves at Leslie's wedding, somewhere near the spot where she would be taking her vows.

I had known I'd be an emotional wreck planning my daughter's wedding, but I wasn't prepared for the enormous jolt into the past —the complete flashback to our life in those times, the absence of a father. Why must it always be the father who's absent? In my life anyway. How Bogie would have loved to be at his daughter's wedding, walking down that aisle. But then, I thought, if he had lived, all our lives would have been different. For one thing, there would have been no Sam. And life without Sam was unthinkable, so forget the ifs. Things were the way they were. Life happens.

Each day was taken up with a new adventure. The manager of the restaurant would handle everything, from a meeting with the chef to the flowers for Leslie, me, and all the rest. My life for that day was in his hands: color scheme white, yellow, and with a touch of lavender. Plants would be rented to transform the backyard into a garden. Rented chairs and a white aisle runner would help cover those portions of lawn where the grass refused to grow.

Mother and daughter were smiling at each other on a regular basis now. We even had some fun times together—a little trousseau shopping. It always pleases me when Leslie sees something she likes and wants. In truth, she doesn't want a great deal. She doesn't want the clutter that I have. She wants one of something, as opposed to ten, which is more my habit.

So all things being unequal, as they are, I left L.A. feeling good about decisions decided upon and my daughter happy and looking beautiful.

No sooner had I returned from L.A. than I had to take off for London to do publicity for a television show I had appeared in some months before; then to Paris for an evening with students at the Sorbonne. So though the wedding continually lurked in the background, I was happy to be in Paris—in my cozy rooms at my favorite Hôtel Duc de St.-Simon—and to spend mornings at the Café Flore with my *International Herald Tribune*, ordering *oeufs à la coque* (boiled eggs to you), *tartine grillé* (a small baguette cut lengthwise and toasted), grapefruit juice, Badoit (natural water), and *café*, occasionally raising my eyes to gaze at passersby: other breakfast eaters, some beer drinkers (yes, in the morning), friendly waiters, and general Left Bank activity. After two weeks of partial work, I returned home to regroup.

A few days after my return, I was obliged to go to Rochester to accept the George Eastman Award for achievement in the arts (awards like this both flatter and confuse me). Then to fly home the following day to present my *Applause* and *Woman of the Year* producer Jimmy Nederlander with his Man of the Year award.

But looming over everything in larger-than-life-size type was the WEDDING: my head crammed with details of the day, and the things I wanted to say to Leslie. Things I had been harboring for many years, dramatically lurking in the background and waiting for this day, plus my terrible fear of being left out, or was it of being taken for granted? It was one of those, and imagined or not, connected to my childhood of omissions or not, it was there and flourishing. At the same time, I was coming to realize what my mother must have felt when I married Bogie. Somewhat bereft—somewhat misplaced—yet encased in endless joy for happiness found.

So the packing began. One suitcase for Leslie. I had kept a

beautiful silver pitcher that was one of the trophies Bogie had won in a sailboat race. I wanted Leslie to have that—engraved with her father's name, the race and year, 1954, when he was healthy and she was two. Also in the suitcase, two cashmere shawls—one for the wedding day, one for after—and various things I'd bought for her in Paris, plus ties for Erich, to choose one for the day.

I had planned on arriving ten days before the wedding, to tie up the final arrangements, and I knew I would need a few days after the wedding to recover. We had agreed that when I was in Los Angeles we would set aside a day to show Leslie the house she had been born into and to give her proof positive that what I claimed to have done some thirty-five years before was a fact: her name and footprints at age two on the swimming pool steps. And there were those magnolia leaves.

I brought caviar from Zabar's; had to hand-carry it. If I was not schlepping something, it would not be me. Someday (in the next life, I fear), I want to travel someplace without carrying anything more than a book.

At last I was on my way. Leslie had told me what afternoons she was free to go to the house and do other last-minute things with me. She would be teaching until a few days before the wedding.

I boarded the plane, excited, nervous, very happy for Leslie, and with a head full of memories. Memories are insidious little things. I never thought I would devote much time to them, being, as I have always claimed, a champion of the present, a creature of now. I remember often resenting Bogie's sometime preoccupation with "the good old days." I suppose I saw little point in dwelling on what was over and never to come again, losing precious today time on yesterday, and also I was probably a little jealous of days I was not part of, knew nothing of. But in fact, memories are lovely things to have, to call upon from time to time. They can be a comfort. At this time—as I was airborne—they were more than a comfort. They were company.

From the moment the airplane touched down at LAX, apprehensions and nerves notwithstanding, I knew everything was going to be all right. I had not only made the decision to behave myself, go with the flow, try to relax; I meant it. That accomplished, the doing of it all became easier.

Steve and Barbara were arriving the following day, and we all planned to be at the airport to meet them. They were expecting Leslie and Erich but not the rest of us; we would be the surprise. I was more than anxious to see my elder son, who was so vulnerable now after some recent illnesses. We hid behind a pillar at the airport gate, except for Sam, who stood out front with "Bogart" written in big black letters on an envelope, limo driver style.

It was so marvelous to see Steve jump right in and take an active part in his sister's wedding, wanting to be part of the planning and doing of all things leading up to and including the approaching day. He'd always loved Leslie, always worried about her being alone, but for many years they had lived in different states, pursuing different ways of life. To see them together meant a great deal to me, as did seeing Steve and Sam together. Children, as those of you who have them know, are all different: they want different things, respond in different ways, live differently. They each go through their bad times and good times, often not together. Having grown up solo—no brothers or sisters—I was determined to have children, not a child. I wanted to know that no matter what, they would have each other. Family would not let you down; my mother's teachings had never left me. As my three have led such independent lives and have had varied emotional crises in their lives, it is a miracle to me that they enjoy being together and are basically as close as they are. I am so grateful for it. What I had always prayed for had finally happened. I saw it unfold, from Steve's arrival to his departure four days later. And was it ever a good thing to see.

Now I must go back a couple of days—to the moment when Leslie and I returned to Mapleton Drive, where we lived for six years and where Bogie died.

My heart was pounding as we entered the driveway and stood waiting for the front door to open. I was so anxious for Leslie to remember something about the house. I was too anxious, bound to be disappointed. Ray Stark, who has been the owner since 1959, let us in. There was a butler standing at attention, looking not unlike the butler we had had. Yes, we actually had a butler! I kept peeking at Leslie to see if I could find a glimmer of recognition in her face. Of course, I couldn't.

We walked into the lanai, a large sun room much frequented by us in those good old days, then headed for the garden and pool. At last I was able to show her, and see again myself, what I'd only told her about these many years. On approaching our own personal footprints in cement, I had a flash of the day we did it—wet gray cement on a day glistening with the California sun. On close scrutiny, the footprints had mostly worn away. I detected a shadow of some, though I'm still not sure whether it was an optical illusion or not. But the names Leslie and Stephen Bogart were clearly in view. So she saw them: that was reality, I had not invented it, it happened.

Amazingly, the Japanese gardener who had worked for us from time to time was still there. He'd cut the magnolia leaves for the wedding, said hello, remembered me and remembered Leslie. It was not the same garden, however. Ray Stark had a beautiful sculpture garden, with Henry Moore, Maillol, Marini, Manzu, and others strategically placed. But the setting was the same. Sam met us there. He wasn't certain he should, feeling it might be a time for Leslie and me. But I wanted him to see it; he'd heard about it often enough. It was eerie being in that house again. Though it looked very different—the color scheme, the decor—it was completely familiar to me. I saw every piece of furniture I had bought, placed where I had placed it. Those walls that had reverberated with sounds of laughter, barking dogs, and babies' cries, and with tears and pain. That beautiful house, which had been such a happy one and then so terribly sad. We left with a car overflowing with magnolia leaves. Leslie's memory was unjarred. She only said she felt it all to be very familiar. It's hard—no, impossible—to know if she has buried it so deep that it cannot be brought forth again, whether "familiar" is truly all there is or perhaps all she wants it to be.

I had a lovely antique necklace that Leslie had always admired, and I had often said, "You'll get it on your wedding day." I brought it to California. She had completely forgotten about it, so that when I presented it to her on that Saturday, in the only hour of private time we had together, she was thrilled. We fell into conversation about life—love—marriage—and of our mother-daughter relationship throughout her life. I had the conversation all figured out. I had wanted to tell her how much I loved her, how proud I was of the woman she had become, how aware I was of our sometime personality problems with each other, will against will; to talk to her about what I felt for her and about her as she was about to embark on a whole new life, to be shared permanently with someone else, a life unlike any she had experienced before. Plans never work out, do they? Particularly when based on emotions. I had been thinking of her as a girl in her twenties, taking off in life for the first time, not fully realizing that she was thirty-eight and had learned a great deal already and certainly knew what she didn't want. She wasn't my little girl anymore, even though she would always be my little girl.

I took a good look at her. What a beauty she was—is. A mixed-up face: part Bogie, part me, part her, resulting in a completely original Leslie face. She still had a great innocence about her. Though she thought marriage would not change her relationship with Erich, since they had been living together for a year, I knew that it would. When you are two people, you look to your future with greater confidence and can conceivably plan for it. And you've said those words, taken those vows, before witnesses.

I gradually realized that after thirty-eight years of conversations with, living with, worrying about Leslie—arguing with her too, of course—I would never again approach her in quite the same way. We talked of her father, and I told her, though she already knew, how very much I wanted a sense of his presence at her wedding. I wanted it as much for myself as I did for her, I realize now. It made me feel less alone. We all know we love our children and our children love us, but the facts are that when they grow up (and they can't wait to do that), get married, and have their own families, they are off and running with their own lives. They want us there—or to know we are there somewhere—but their lives come first. Mine did. How did my mother feel? As bereft, extraneous as I did? Because my children—all of them—were couples now. So face it: alone is alone is alone. It's very real and very apparent when the last of your children finds a mate. Your thinking must be rearranged. Except for the fact that it's never done, to all intents and purposes my work was done. They each had their significant other. I am their independent, significant mother, more separated from them than ever before. Though the mother figure never dies, it fades into the background until brought up short and into vivid life through illness or death.

Of course, I had to feel Bogie's presence—of course, he was with me waking and sleeping. Often before, but more than ever at this time. He and I had made this girl.

My sons' marriages affected me differently. My daughter was my only girl; I was my mother's only child. My daughter was me at twenty when I got married. That explained so much of my attitude, my confused feelings toward Leslie those days before the wedding. How history repeats itself—how generations do. How long it takes to begin to figure it out—to figure anything out. I thought I was so smart, but I missed that one.

On the Sunday morning, after threatened rain, the sun shone. Thank God, I thought (superstitious me): "Happy is the bride the sun shines on." I had slept fitfully, woke early. Leslie had been saying she wasn't nervous.

When I arrived at Leslie's, she was in her tights and camisole—hair done, wearing my diamond earrings lent for the occasion, the necklace I had given her—and about to climb into her dress. Her neighbor was steaming it; there was a lot of scattered talk. She looked beautiful: radiant, face aglow. Her dress and jacket were a triumph. Simple and beautiful; a perfect choice.

I felt pride in her, a rush of love for her, sad that Bogie was not there—so alive in my memory, so dim in hers—happy that she had found happiness at last, and sad again that there was only me. I

Leslie on her wedding day—the faces speak for themselves.

had pictured those storybook photos of the bride and her father arriving together, with him the one to walk her down the aisle and hand her over to her soon-to-be husband. Instead of which there was the bride and her mother arriving together, not the same thing at all; later, me walking down the aisle with Erich's father, as I had welcoming words to say, given to me by the man performing the ceremony. They were few and lovely words, simple. Erich's father was to light a candle and strike a gong, then Leslie and Erich were to enter and walk down the aisle together.

When we arrived at Sam's, some friends of Erich's, who had arrived early, were standing outside the house. Leslie stopped to say hello. I headed her inside the house, asked them to please go to the back garden, where the ceremony was to take place. Knotted stomach; my last chance to inflict my traditional ideas on this day: there was no best man, no maid of honor, but I was damned if I was going to allow everyone to see the bride before the wedding. The few that walked into the house were firmly sent outdoors. Steve and Sam were to direct people as they arrived. Erich was coming last and was not to set eyes upon Leslie until about fifteen minutes before the ceremony, when they would do and say whatever they had planned to do and say alone together.

The lama who was performing the ceremony was a nice-looking young man in a business suit, who looked nothing at all like my imagined Tibetan priest. Little by little, I found myself waking up to the differences in Leslie and Erich's way of life. How different their thinking was from mine, yet I think I was beginning to understand it. Neither of them is a Buddhist, but they live very much in the yoga world, which is a world foreign to me. I know how very much it has helped her, and the more exposed to it I am, the more certain I am that some of it would be good for all of us.

The ceremony was filled with promise, purpose, loyalty, devotion, and hope for the future and for the rest of their lives. I don't know what I expected. Having heard "Tibetan priest," I suppose I thought there might be some weirdness, proving once again how ignorance distorts.

I was moved, thinking of those vows, of what those words meant. How hopeful we all are at the beginning; how hopeful—no, how certain—I was at both my marriage ceremonies. It all seems so easy, to be able to live those vows, but how difficult and complicated it can become when life gets in the way. I didn't cry, as I did at Sam's wedding, but I was very tremulous. And Steve, sweet Steve, reached out and took my hand and held it throughout the ceremony. Such an overt gesture for him. I don't think he had done anything like that since he was a little boy. I hoped he had been thinking of his father too. His hand gave me strength and reassurance and was something I shall never forget. Steve had also been put in charge of passing the multicolored rice, so it could be thrown at Mr. and Mrs. as they walked up the aisle. He was so nervous that when there was a pause in the ceremony, he thought it was over and proceeded to stand up—ready to pass the rice, clearly afraid of missing the right moment. He was hurriedly told to wait, tiny giggles were heard in various quarters. He was irresistible that day.

The next thing I knew, the ring was being called for. Erich promptly dropped it, having held on to it throughout so as not to have to fish for it. Now it came unstuck from his finger and headed for the carpet. He retrieved it quickly, and the ring went on Leslie's finger without a hitch. Then it was her turn—not to drop it but to fumble a bit—and he was kissing her. Then they were officially sealed, though she remains Leslie Bogart.

The step had been taken. She was already visibly involved with another family and other friends. She was on her way. And I realized that even though I was mother and she daughter, when she had been on her own and I would see her with some of her friends, we all got along so well that in some strange way I almost felt like a contemporary of theirs, though my head told me differently. But then I—and of course Sam and Steve—was her only family. Now she would be shared.

The reception was filled with roughly eighty of Leslie's and Erich's friends and family and ten of mine: a resounding success. I toasted my daughter, telling all present how happy I was that she had waited for Erich, what a wonder she was, and how proud her father would have been to see her this day. But though I am happy for her and filled with joy that she has a wonderful life ahead, I discover to my amazement that her marriage has been something of a jolt for me. And I wondered if Steve was right when he looked at me after the ceremony and said, "Well, Mom, she's the last one. Now you're next."

Maybe.

But meanwhile the unthinkable has happened. The union of Sam and Suzy has finally fallen victim to the insurmountable obstacle of the "business." Too many separations; careers and marriage do not mix, at least not the careers that send you off traveling in ten opposite directions. And people change. I had sensed it coming for the last couple of years but had chosen to turn my back on it.

I remembered London almost nine years ago, and the declarations of love coming from my twenty-three-year-old son. How sure he was—how open—how happy. How dedicated they were, he and Suzy, each to the other. How certain they were that they would go on forever. And then I remembered how people change, how needs change, and how different life looks with each passing year. How what you thought—no, you were positive—you could handle, you find you can't. It's more pain than you ever want to see your child have to bear. I do know how difficult being married can be and how constant attention must be paid—but I also know that only living experience can teach you that. Steve has found his happiness in a solid second marriage; Leslie waited until she was sure. I'm certain Sam, too, will find his way to a new and satisfying life.

# STILL BY MYSELF

How odd it seems—is—to arrive at the realization that I have been living alone, traveling solo, not been half of a pair, a couple, since October of 1969. How can it be? Is it possible? How have I managed all these years? It is time to look back to see why—to see if it might have been different, if it could have been?

After an unhappy second marriage, I had my very first taste of single blessedness. I was free—well, almost—with one small child, one teenager, and one twenty-year-old. I didn't want a serious relationship, a long-term one; I really didn't want anything specifically to do with another human being—a man. I wanted to work. My energy, my emotion, went into my work. But as emotion plays such an enormous part in my profession, it was only natural to become involved, to almost fall in love, to think I was in love (which is almost as good). At that point in my life and for the ten years after, being a romantic fool, I fell in love, or thought I had fallen, a couple of times. That clearly is my nature—not what motivates me but a large and necessary part of me. To feel. The relationships didn't work out. I talked about two of them in my autobiography. One went on for quite a long time —was based, I think, on working together on a daily basis, on mutual attraction and having fun. Still, it was complicated and became emotionally difficult for me. The other was passionate, possessed, impossible, and bad news. Ironically, after Bogie, both men were a good deal younger than I was.

Younger men seem to be braver, more spontaneous than older types. At least at the beginning. It's not an easy thing for a woman to be perceived as strong, infallible, always in control, as is the case with me. I continually have to rise above that. Any man who is drawn to me must have the willingness, curiosity, and sensitivity to move beyond those perceptions. In my experience, younger men have been more willing to do that, even eager. While older men seem to need constant reassurance—ego building—from young women, younger men may want whatever intelligence and experience an older woman can provide. They are attracted to what my life has been and might be. Now, I am not interested in being somebody's mother or sister. I love being treated as a woman—even a sex object. That's what makes me feel fabulous: puts the roses in my cheeks, the sparkle in my eyes. That's what makes me feel I have a future with a man. That's *the* great feeling. Why the hell it should be thought that I need less than any other woman is beyond me. Or do they think I need more? Or do they think?

Male-female relationships are such fragile, often unexpected things. Most of mine have been born either of work, thereby forcing proximity, or from having to be somewhere for a professional reason. I have never met anyone at a social event whom I wanted to see more than twice.

Timing, of course, is the element we have no control over. And timing has everything to do with the direction relationships take. They happen one year instead of another for no apparent reason other than that you must have been open to them. Often you've heard of two people who've known each other for years—paid no attention to each other, just casual friends—then, five, ten years later, whammo!

They meet again, fall in love, get married, and live happily ever after. There's no figuring.

I never stopped to try to see if I was happy. How would I know? What is happy, anyway? The more you know, the more you see, the more elusive "happy" becomes. Sometimes yes, sometimes no. But over all, on reflection, I would say no. I denied that part of myself, stopped thinking about it, about love: the emotion, the feeling of wanting, of being wanted—of giving to and doing for someone else, of sharing, of being interested in and by another. As the years passed, I guess, I subliminally decided that perhaps I didn't need to have those feelings—not even sex. Sex for me has always mattered not for its own sake but as part of loving a man, wanting to be with a certain man physically, a man I could also talk to. I didn't reason it out. I was too busy. Work has been primo—taking up most of my focus, my time, my energy—my children and friends took the rest. But always in the back of my mind was the thought that one day, unexpectedly, that man would appear who would interest me, stimulate me, attract me. These things happen when they are meant to. I suppose, finally, that to a large degree I am a fatalist.

And also I have seen so much pain, anger, frustration, and neglect in marriage and relationships that I have been rather turned off. I've thought and I've said/joked aloud, "Who needs this?" I've done my bit—made my contribution to humanity, had my children. And I've traveled the world over. I've looked everywhere: where are they, these men? I've looked under tables, chairs, in cupboards, under beds, *in* beds. You name it; I've looked. I have not found. They are a rare, elusive breed. So what's a girl to do? Forget it—hopeless. Still, when I observe (and it's so rare as to be almost nonexistent) two people who really like each other, really enjoy each other, nothing on earth looks better to me. Sure, my needs have altered over the last twenty years—even ten—and/or I have shoved them under the rug, out of sight. My body has shifted, though I take fairly good care of it; I find myself aware of parts I always took for granted, like my toes, my eyes, my ears. It's infuriating to have a part of you suddenly work less well.

It's unacceptable. But time does have a way of interfering. And who knows how many years are ahead anyway? Maybe ten—maybe twenty —maybe five. I pass lightly and quickly over those numbers.

But recently I have actually experienced a new awakening —a sense of it being possible, of there being someone for me to love. Somewhere. The truth is that love is the best feeling to have in this world. And the truth also is . . . I miss it. I *want* to have somebody's hand to hold. I *want* to have someone to laugh with, someone who wants what I want. I want someone to tell me I look great, and mean it. Only lately have I realized how long, for how many years, I've been closed to that emotion. How I have almost behaved as though it didn't exist—was unnecessary. Not consciously, I suspect; just to avoid dealing with the fact of nobody being there.

If the distraction wasn't a movie, it was a lecture; if not a lecture, a possible homage. If none of the above, I'd get on a plane to Paris, to London, for some drummed-up reason. Any move to quell my restlessness.

I am still restless—will ever be, I fear. Nevertheless, I'm ready for the next emotional adventure. I don't want to be alone anymore. Not all the time. And I know now I won't be. Just as I know I can be as giddy, as excited today as ever I was at nineteen.

When I was a little girl I read fairy tales. I dreamed of being Cinderella. I grew up imagining—fantasizing—with an obviously tremendous need to love and be loved, to be carried off to a dream house by a dream prince. I was a full-blown romantic. I think I dreamed those dreams, was transported to those places, because I had grown up in a loving but exclusively female household where there were no man-woman relationships to emulate. I didn't know what romantic love was all about. But I wanted it—oh, how I wanted it. Imagine what I felt when my prince did arrive! There couldn't have been a more romantic time than Bogie's courtship of me and our first three and a half years together. Gradually I learned how to live with a man —what it meant to share your life. With a nonexistent father in my background, I didn't know that I could ever trust a man. Of course, I learned very quickly that I could trust Bogie; then, painfully, that I could not trust some who followed him. I marvel at the fact that I still believe there might be a man I can trust again. I don't mean only physically, though that counts for a great deal. Womanizing, being predictably one who is unable to build a relationship with one woman and make it stick. To trust your partner, to nourish the partnership—care and feeding being of prime importance. I learned early on the value of a phone call: keeping it alive, keeping it fun. I'll never forget the excitement I felt when I heard the key turn in the lock of the front door; or when the call came at the expected hour; when the kiss became an enveloping desire. Those feelings—the catching of breath —I refuse to believe will never come again. And the greatest gift is the sharing of laughter. I cannot fathom a life without laughter. All my life I have had, with a bow to Noël Coward, a talent to amuse. My consistent gift has been to make men laugh. That might not be such a good or deliberate quality—to the men, that is. But to me, to be in love with a man and to share laughter is the best possible combination of emotions. For me ideal, for me necessary.

The strange thing is that as you grow older, along with knowledge, the pain of losses, the changes in your life, in your work, even the physical changes we all unhappily must experience—the thickening of the waist, the lines, the sags—even with all that and more, you don't stop wanting and needing to recapture the feelings you had when you began. I haven't stopped: that's the great surprise of life. And the great hope—the unknown factor that keeps you going, no matter how black the future seems at times. The not knowing what may be waiting for you around the corner. The fact that with each ending comes a new beginning. I think to myself from time to time, "Are you crazy? Don't be ridiculous, you idiot, you're not a schoolgirl. Grow up! Those things won't happen to you now." The hell they won't! Why not? Who is to say what anyone's prime is? Who decides that you stop feeling, stop yearning? In America the general perception is that at a certain age everything stops. In my profession, at twenty you're a sexpot; at thirty, you're still playing romantic leads; at thirty-five you start looking over your shoulder to see who's chasing you . . . then the comeback trail starts, and that is one thing that never stops.

By the time you reach fifty, sex becomes meaningless, the drive is gone, the invisible "they" say. At sixty, finding love is just about impossible. Who started these rumors? Who made these decisions? Who says you stop feeling? Why should you? Why does a number justify the end of emotion? Why should you be written off by others, until finally you do it yourself? For myself, I look forward to the next adventure, which may not be the last love affair in my life. And I thank God for that, because it is love that keeps your heart beating faster.

And yet, even so, the seduction of being alone is ever present and strong. The older you get, the more alone you become, and the more seductive it becomes. The doing as you please, the answering to no one, the dinner on a tray, the morning silence—all that argues against the need to be with someone. Yet the need keeps on rearing its needy head.

The great enemy of us all—time—will deprive me of ever having a silver anniversary. But as I have spent so many of my years in the world of "pretend," I hope that when Mr. Right appears on the scene, I will be able to pretend that one year equals five. In that way perhaps I can even have a golden anniversary.

But whatever happens, in my life—in love, sex, marriages —I at least have been lucky enough to have known it all, the good, the bad, and the ugly. Even the bad had a positive side. For a while, burying personal, immediate gratification, I was freed to pursue and develop the creativity that was mine alone, a good deal of which had been buried while I tried to preserve a relationship. Let's face it: I want it all—just like you and everybody else. It may not be in the cards, but the prospect is so dazzling that I have to try.

After Leslie's wedding, something odd happened to me. Imperceptibly, insidiously, a kind of resentment came over me. At first I thought it was because I had not felt appreciated, that Leslie had not realized what had erupted within me, reaching a climax on that day. The anger I felt was directed at Leslie because the reality of my being the last and only one left hit me so hard. But it was not only that—it was my fury with myself at feeling so lost, at needing so much more than I had thought I did. Wondering how much future lies ahead. Asking myself where and how do I want to spend the next ten, fifteen, twenty years? What do I really want? After all these years of living, I still don't have the answers. Or even *an* answer.

It's partially the travel—the amount of it—that keeps me from facing the pluses and minuses. Too much introspection can be a big mistake, finally boring, to me and to everyone else. Life is to be lived, not analyzed. Time is to be used, not wasted. And all of it is nonstop adjusting to new and different aches and pains, to change— change of mind, change of body—and to other people, including and especially one's children, who are also changing. It seems to me, what with time's terrifying knack of moving so quickly, that I've almost missed a chunk of my life, that during these last years—between acting jobs—there has been too much reflection and reassessment. Though on close examination they have been only intermittent. And though it might be accepted as fairly normal after sixty, there hasn't been enough time to indulge. Thank God.

In my apartment of more than thirty years, I am surrounded by my life. My several lives. I look around me. Going from room to room, I am faced with one or more of my collections, my follies: books, pewter, brass, Delft, majolica, tables, chairs, *things*, each representing a special age—a marriage, a change in taste, a shifting of some kind. I remember clearly where I was and when each piece was bought. Even so, how did it happen, the acquiring of all this, the accumulation of it? Now that I have it all, what do I do with it? Who will want it? My children are not collectors; their needs are not what mine were. Certainly not what mine are. So slowly I am beginning to sort out; time to get rid of things. Clothes to the Fashion Institute, the Lighthouse; furniture I have no need for: first to my children, then anywhere. That doesn't even include what must be organized: papers, endless papers, letters, clippings, notes, photos to be sorted out. What to keep, what to throw away? The will. The endless list-making—what to give to whom. Difficult enough with three children. Suppose I'd had six?

So what is all this planning and disposing of things about?

It's about restlessness. It's about letting go. About not being smothered by things. It's about my three great children, whom I not only adore but admire and respect. And their small children: my grandchildren, whose growth I can observe as they stumble through their school years and with whom I may have some kind of relationship.

Yet they are, each of them, focused on their own worlds, and I am not part of that.

I wonder if I will ever love anyone again or if anyone will ever love me. I know how lucky I have been to once have had in my life a man who loved me without reservation and whom I loved in the same way. But that was long ago. Can it happen again? Will it? I hope so.

Will I live in this same apartment for whatever my forever will be? Or should I move? Will it be Paris—my heart's city? Where will the work take me? There has to be work. It's my basic need, my structure; it keeps me in shape, my head working, a smile on my face and hope in my heart.

What comes next? I'm not sure, but I feel it's time for a move of some sort, some kind of big change. As for the future: I'll go on believing there is one—maybe even a happy one. Who's to say there is nothing waiting for me around the corner? A new job . . . a new relationship . . . a new home . . . Whatever it may be, one thing is for sure—this adventure is not over.